GCSE RELIGIOUS STUDIES for AQA

CHRISTIAN BELIEF AND PRACTICE:

THE ROMAN CATHOLIC TRADITION

Gordon Geddes
Jane Griffiths

D1581809

Heinemann Educational Publishers
Halley Court, Jordan Hill, Oxford, OX2 8EJ
Part of Harcourt Education

Heinemann is a registered trademark of
Harcourt Education Limited

First published in 2002

06
10 9 8 7 6 5

British Library Cataloguing in Publication Data
A catalogue record for this book is available from the
British Library

10-digit ISBN: 0 435 30691 X
13-digit ISBN: 978 0 435 30691 5

Picture research by Jennifer Johnson
Designed and typeset by Artistix, Oxon
Illustrations by Andrew Skilleter
Printed and bound in Italy by Printer Trento S.R.L.

Acknowledgements
The publishers would like to thank the following for
permission to reproduce copyright material:
Church House Publishing for The Apostles' Creed, p. 10;
Faber & Faber for the extract from 'The Journey of the
Magi' from Collected Poems 1909–1962 by T. S. Eliot,
p. 95; Jubilate Hymns for 'Wise Men they came to look for
wisdom' © Christopher Idle/Jubilate Hymns, p. 95; Kevin
Mayhew for 'Love is his word' from Hymns Old and New,
p. 45; Basil E. Bridges for 'Lord of love and life', p. 86.

Cover photograph by Mary Evans Picture Library

The publishers would like to thank the following for
permission to use photographs:
Ancient Art and Architecture, p. 3; Andes Press
Agency/Carlos Reyes-Manzo, pp. 9, 18, 25, 31, 34, 35,
42, 43, 44, 45, 47, 48, 49, 52, 58, 59, 60, 62, 69, 70,
73, 74, 79, 80, 85, 88, 89, 92, 99 and 107; The Art
Archive, p. 59; The Art Archive/British Library, p. 38; The
Art Archive/Tate Gallery London/Ellen Tweedy, p. 102;
Gareth Boden, p. 81; The Bridgeman Art Library, p. 15;
The Bridgeman Art Library/Lauros-Giraudon, p. 13;
Camera Press/Rota, p. 103; CIRCA/John Fryer, pp. 106
and 113; CIRCA Photo Library, p. 28; CIRCA/John Smith,
p. 107; Evangelische Kirchengemeinde, p. 95; Gordon
Geddes, pp. 55 and 95; Glasgow Museums: The St
Mungo Museum of Religious Life and Art, p. 105; Robert
Harding/D Hughes, p. 29; Robert Harding/P Craven,
p. 20; Robert Harding/Caroline Wood/Int'l Stock, p. 77;
Impact/Mohamed Ansar, p. 18; Impact/Eliza Armstrong,
p. 29; Impact/Alan Blair, p. 38; Impact/Piers Cavendish,
p. 32; Impact/Geraint Lewis, p. 18; Impact/Caroline Penn,
p. 110; John Ryland Library, University of Manchester,
p. 3; Mary Evans Picture Library, p. 8; Panos Pictures/
Howard Davies, p. 56; Photodisc, pp. 8 and 65; Zed
Radovan, pp. 40, 41 and 54; Science Photo Library/Jim
Gipe/Agstock, p. 82; Graham Snape, pp. 67, 68 and 91;
Sonia Halliday Photographs, pp. 41, 110 and 112; Sonia
Halliday Photographs/FHC Birch, p. 60; Sonia Halliday
Photographs/Bryan Knox, pp. 5 and 91; Sonia Halliday
Photographs/Laura Lushington, p. 64; Sonia Halliday
Photographs/Patrick Reyntiens, p. 61; Sonia Halliday
Photographs/David Silverman, p. 100; Sonia Halliday
Photographs/Jane Taylor, p. 33; Fr David Yates, p. 39.

The publishers have made every effort to contact
copyright holders. However, if any material has been
incorrectly acknowledged, the publishers would be
pleased to correct this at the earliest opportunity.

Tel: 01865 888058 www.heinemann.co.uk

Contents

Christian initiation

Other rites of passage

The Christmas cycle of festivals

The Easter cycle of festivals

Notes for teachers

Welcome! We hope this book will be a useful resource in teaching GCSE students.

What this book contains

This book is designed to support AQA's GCSE option of specification A for Religious Studies – Christian Belief and Practice with reference to the Roman Catholic Tradition.

It is divided into eight sections and provides full coverage of the specification. Within each section there is a series of self-contained units. The units include illustrations and key points to summarize the main learning points. At the end of each section there are exam tips and practice questions, and support for coursework is provided on pages 115–18.

Key terms in the specification are explained the first time they appear in the book. Other difficult words and phrases can be found in the glossary on pages 119–20 and are written in bold the first time they appear in a section. Extracts from the Bible have been taken from the New International Version.

How to use this book

As far as possible we have followed the order of topics as contained in the specification. Teachers will decide for themselves whether this is the order in which they would like to teach the specification.

Activities

Suggested activities, which are mainly discussion or individual research topics, are given at the end of each unit. The activities are designed to develop knowledge and understanding of the specification content. They can also be used to develop Key Skills and have been coded to show which Key Skill they might develop.

Some activities make use of the following drama techniques.

- Thought-tracking – working in pairs or groups of three, students reconstruct an event. They use a handclap signal to indicate the change from speech to thought and back again. Others in the group can reply to speech but not to thought.
- Hot seat – the teacher or a student in role sits in the hot seat and has questions asked of them relating to their character. This technique can be used as exploration (with the teacher in role providing facts as answers), as revision (same format) when the questions become more important than the answers, or with a student in role helping to organise thoughts.
- Forum theatre – a scene is enacted and watched by the rest of the group, who can intervene to freeze the action, ask for clarification, add thought, take over a character or add another.

These techniques are well-known to teachers of Drama. Some Religious Education teachers may wish to consult Drama colleagues for more advice about how to use them.

We have been careful to cover assessment objectives AO1, AO2 and AO3. However, in the coursework section we have not used these terms with students but have made the ideas more accessible by referring to knowledge, understanding and evaluation.

Notes for students

Welcome! We hope you find this book helpful in your studies.

About your AQA course

This book is designed to support AQA's GCSE option of specification A for Religious Studies – Christian Belief and Practice with reference to the Roman Catholic Tradition.

If you are following a full course, the information in this book covers half the requirements of your GCSE. If you are following a short course, it will cover all your needs.

You will be assessed in two ways. You will have to do coursework (for up to 20 per cent of the marks for the short course and 10 per cent for the full course). You will also have to undergo a written examination at the end of the course (for up to 80 per cent of the marks for the short course and 40 per cent for the full course).

About this book

This book is divided into eight sections and provides full coverage of all the topics in the specification. Within each section there is a series of self-contained units. In each unit you will find illustrations and key points to summarize what you have learnt. At the end of each section there are exam tips and practice questions. On pages 115–18 support for your coursework is provided.

Key terms in the specification are explained the first time they appear in the book. Other difficult words and phrases can be found in the glossary on pages 119–20 and are written in bold the first time they appear in a section.

Hints on exam success

Remember that sound knowledge is the key to success in your GCSE examination. In particular, you must know the contents of the specification accurately and in detail.

Bible references are written as follows.

- John chapter 8, verse 12: (John 8:12).
- Matthew chapter 25, verses 31 to 32: (Matthew 25:31–32).

Note that in exam papers, the various Christian groups (for example, Methodists, Baptists) may be called *either* traditions *or* denominations.

It is important to remember that there are two different ways of marking exam questions.

- Some questions are marked point by point with a mark for each point made. Sometimes two marks may be given for a well-made point or one for a point that is clumsy or incomplete.
- Other questions are marked on levels of response. The examiner assesses the answer as a whole and decides at what level to credit.

Study the following examples.

1   **Question:** What did Jesus say as he gave the bread and wine to his disciples at the Last Supper? *(3 marks)*

    Mark scheme: You would get one mark each for 'This is my body' and 'This is my blood'. As long as the terms 'body' and 'blood' are correctly used, phrases such as 'Here is my body' would be credited. The third mark would be for a further point, for example, 'the New Covenant'.

2   **Question:** Why do some Christians practise believers' baptism? *(4 marks)*

    Mark scheme: To gain marks here you need to make clear that the persons being baptized should be able to understand the meaning of what they are doing. In the light of their understanding they should make a personal decision to commit themselves to following and serving Jesus as their Saviour. They are dying to sin and rising again to new life. This is how an examiner would award marks for this question.

    Level 1: An answer at this level would only contain one or two relevant basic points.

    Level 2: An answer at this level would have some understanding of the meaning of the rite, on a simple level.

    Level 3: At this level the student will have shown awareness not only of the need for understanding but also of the need for choice and/or commitment.

    Level 4: For full marks the answer must cover most, not necessarily all, of the above points.

Beliefs and sources of authority

This section includes:

- The Bible
- How Christians understand the Bible
- The Bible in Christian worship
- The creeds
- The Apostles' Creed
- Mary, Mother of God
- Mary's place in Roman Catholic belief.

The Bible is the Holy Book of Christians. It is divided into two parts: the Old Testament, written before the time of Jesus; and the New Testament, written by the followers of Jesus. Different Christians interpret the Bible in different ways. The Bible is used in many ways as a part of worship.

The creeds are statements of belief. In many traditions the creeds are taken as one of the standards by which Christianity is defined. The Apostles' Creed contains a summary of basic Christian beliefs.

Mary is recognized by Roman Catholics as the Mother of God, a title which stresses that Jesus her son is both divine and human. She is in heaven, praying for the whole human family. Roman Catholics see her as a role model and guide.

The Bible

Key terms

Bible the holy book of Christians

Testament one of the two parts into which the Bible is divided: the Old Testament was written before the time of Jesus and the New Testament was written by followers of Jesus. The basic meaning is 'a binding agreement'

What is the Bible?

The **Bible** is the Christian holy book. The name comes from the Greek word 'biblos' meaning book. Christians speak of the Bible as the Word of God. The Bible is a collection of books written by different people at different times. It is divided into two parts – the Old Testament and the New Testament. The word **testament** means an oath or covenant, a binding promise and agreement. Each part of the Bible describes an agreement made between God and members of the human race.

- The Old Testament is the covenant between God and the Jewish nation. It was sealed by the sacrifice of the Passover lamb (see page 42).
- The New Testament is the covenant between God and the whole of the human race. Christians are people who accept the covenant. It was sealed by the death of Jesus on the cross.

What is in the Old Testament?

- The first book – Genesis – contains accounts of the creation, the flood and the lives of the patriarchs (Abraham, Isaac, Jacob and Joseph – important ancestors of the Jewish people).
- The next four books – Exodus, Leviticus, Numbers and Deuteronomy – are about the life of Moses and the laws given by God through Moses to the people of Israel.
- The Histories. These books describe the history of the Jewish nation from the time of Joshua to the fifth century BC. They also describe the lives of certain individuals. Two books (Ruth and Esther) focus entirely on the women after whom the books are named.

- The Book of Psalms. Psalms are songs of praise and prayer used in worship.
- The Wisdom books. These contain a range of religious and moral teachings, presented in different ways. For example, the Book of Job examines the problem of why there is suffering and tries to see its purpose and meaning. By contrast, the Book of Proverbs contains several sayings about many aspects of life.
- The **Prophets**. Prophets are people who speak out in the name of God. The books of the prophets contain some of their messages. The books also describe how some prophets faced difficulties and dangers because they spoke out so bravely. Sometimes prophets have foretold the future, but saying what would or might happen is not their main function.

The books of the Old Testament were written before the time of Jesus. They are the scriptures of the Jews. The first five books are known as the Torah (the Law of Moses), even though they contain much more than laws.

Christians see the Old Testament as leading up to the coming of Jesus. For centuries God was preparing the Jewish people for the coming of the **Messiah**. Christians believe that Jesus is the promised Messiah.

What is in the New Testament?

- The four gospels. These were written by Matthew, Mark, Luke and John.
- The Acts of the Apostles tells how Peter, Paul and others spread Christianity through the Eastern Mediterranean area as far as Rome.
- Letters from Paul, John, Peter and other Christian leaders to Church members in different places.
- Revelation, John's vision of heaven.

The books of the New Testament were written by Jesus' followers in the years after his resurrection.

The gospels are of the greatest importance to Christians. These four books describe the life, teaching, death and resurrection of Jesus. At **Holy Communion** services in many traditions everybody stands for readings from the gospels, in honour of Jesus.

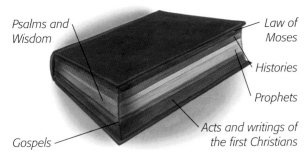

Psalms and Wisdom

Law of Moses

Histories

Prophets

Gospels

Acts and writings of the first Christians

How the Bible is made up

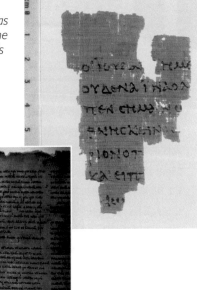

This piece of papyrus, which has on each side some words from John's Gospel, is nearly 1900 years old.

This copy of the Book of Isaiah is more than 2000 years old.

Why are there different versions of the Bible?

The Old Testament is written in Hebrew. The New Testament is written in Greek. Not everyone can read Hebrew and Greek. So, most Christians read the Bible in translation. Translations are always made using the original Hebrew and Greek. It is not true that the words of the Bible have become so changed over the years that the original words have been lost. It is very important to Christians that the words of the Bible have been accurately preserved.

The various translations are different because people naturally use different words. For example, imagine two pupils translating the French phrase, 'Je peux lire.' One might say, 'I can read.' The other might say, 'I am able to read.' The two translations are different but they are both right.

The following are two versions of a saying of Jesus from Matthew's Gospel (6: 3).

- But when you give to the needy, do not let your left hand know what your right hand is doing, so that your giving may be in secret (*New International Version*).

- But when you help a needy person, do it in such a way that even your closest friend will not know about it. Then it will be a private matter (*Good News Bible*).

The New International Version *translates* what Jesus said. The Good News Bible *explains* what Jesus meant.

The Bible is authentic

Why are Christians sure that the words of the Bible have not been changed over the years?

- The words of the Bible have been very carefully preserved to keep the original words unchanged.

- Some copies, or parts of copies, go back almost to the time when the books were first written. The fact that these ancient copies exist shows that the books of the Bible cannot have been written centuries later.

Activities

1 Read these passages from the Old Testament: Exodus 33: 18–23, Psalm 24, Proverbs 10: 1–5, Isaiah 1: 14–18. What did the people who wrote these verses think God was like? **PS 2.1**

2 Read Luke 1: 1–4 and John 21: 24–5. What do these verses tell us about why Luke and John wrote their gospels? **PS 2.1**

Key points

- The Bible is divided into the Old Testament (written before the time of Jesus) and the New Testament (written by the followers of Jesus).

- The versions of the Bible in use today are accurate translations of what was written thousands of years ago.

How Christians understand the Bible

Key terms

Conservatives people who believe the Bible was inspired by God but is not a scientific text

Fundamentalists people who believe that the Bible was inspired by God and cannot contain errors

Liberals people who believe that, most importantly, the Bible contains spiritual truth

Literalists fundamentalists who believe in the exact literal interpretation of the scripture

The Word of God

Christians believe that the Bible is the Word of God. They believe that God inspired the people who wrote the books of the Bible. When they say 'the Word of God', various Christians mean different things. In particular, they disagree about:

- in what sense it comes from God
- how God influenced the people who wrote it
- in what ways it is true
- how people today should understand it.

Your specification requires you to know the ways in which the Bible is interpreted by **literalists**, **fundamentalists**, **conservatives** and **liberals**:

- Literalists believe in the exact literal interpretation of the scripture in every detail. It is from God and is true in every way.
- Fundamentalists believe that the Bible is completely inspired by God and cannot contain errors. Where there are apparent contradictions, people do not yet have enough understanding, either of the text or of the truth.
- Conservatives believe that the Bible was inspired by God but is not a scientific text. Occasionally there may be difficulties with a text where understanding is not clear. A study of the time and circumstances when the passage was written often makes the meaning clearer.
- Liberals believe that, most importantly, the Bible contains spiritual truth. Like conservatives, they believe that a study of the background to scriptures can make the meaning clearer.

They accept that the writers of the Bible, though guided by God, may have made mistakes.

Read this passage from the opening chapter of Genesis, the first book of the Bible. It is an account of the creation of the world. Then read the interpretations that follow.

> In the beginning God created the heavens and the earth. Now the earth was formless and empty, darkness was over the surface of the deep, and the Spirit of God was hovering over the waters. And God said, 'Let there be light,' and there was light. God saw that the light was good, and he separated the light from the darkness. God called the light 'day', and the darkness he called 'night'. And there was evening, and there was morning – the first day.
>
> God created human beings in his own image, in the image of God he created them; male and female he created them. God blessed them and said to them, 'Be fruitful and increase in number; fill the earth and subdue it. Rule over the fish of the sea and the birds of the air and over every living creature that moves on the ground.' Then God said, 'I give you every seed-bearing plant on the face of the whole earth and every tree that has fruit with seed in it. They will be yours for food. And to all the beasts of the earth and all the birds of the air and all the creatures that move on the ground – everything that has the breath of life in it – I give every green plant for food.' And it was so. God saw all that he had made, and it was very good. And there was evening, and there was morning – the sixth day. (Genesis 1: 1–5, 27–31)

- Literalists take this passage as literally true in every point, believing, for example, that 'day' means precisely 24 hours.
- Fundamentalists believe the account is true, though the words must be properly interpreted. 'Day' here could mean 'a period of time'.
- Conservatives say the writers of Genesis faithfully recorded what people at the time believed to be true. It accurately says that God is

the creator of the universe and gave the human race a unique place in his creation.

- Liberals regard the historical or scientific statements in the passage as irrelevant. The passage is there to illustrate truth about, for instance, th.e basic goodness of creation.

God is the central character

All Christians believe that the Bible is more than an ordinary history. The Bible is about God. God is the central character throughout the Bible.

The Bible only makes sense to people who have faith. It is one thing to believe that an event in the Bible happened. It takes *faith* to believe that God caused it to happen. It takes *faith* to believe that God spoke to someone or guided someone.

Christians believe that God can speak to people through the Bible. As they read the Bible, they understand more about God. They may come to realize that God has a special message for them.

'It was Hezekiah who blocked the upper outlet of the Gihon spring and channelled the water down to the west side of the city of David' (2 Chronicles 32: 30). The discovery of the channel may prove that this chapter is as accurate as history. Other discoveries may prove that Hezekiah was a wealthy king. But no archaeological discovery can ever prove a saying such as 'God had given him very great riches' (2 Chronicles 32: 29). That remains a matter of faith.

The channel that Hezekiah made in Jerusalem.

Lives rooted in the Bible

Many Christians regularly read and study the Bible. They use it in their worship. They want to know more of God and of the life and teaching of Jesus Christ. They want guidance in the way they should live.

A life changed through the Bible

John Dodd was a prisoner of the Japanese for three and a half years during the Second World War. Soon after his release he went to his local Methodist church. The reading from the prophet, Joel, included the words, 'I will repay you for the years the locusts have eaten.'

Joel was writing about a plague of locusts, which had happened over 2000 years ago. John Dodd took the words as a message from God to mean, 'I will give you back those wasted years.' He dedicated his life to other people who were having to cope with getting back to normal life after years as prisoners. He founded the Langley House Trust, an organization that helps people coming out of prison.

Activities

1 Visit the website of the Gideons (www.gideons.org) to learn about how and why they distribute copies of the scriptures. Make notes in preparation for Activity 2. **IT 2.1, 2.2, PS 2.1, 2.2**

2 Hot seat activity: the teacher takes the role of a Gideon (or a Gideon is invited to visit the class). Students question the person in the hot seat on what is so important about the Bible. **C 2.1a, 2.1b**

Key points

- Christians believe the Bible is the Word of God.
- 'The Word of God' means different things to different Christians.
- Many Christians find the Bible gives them guidance.

The Bible in Christian worship

Why do Christians use the Bible?

Christians use the Bible for a number of reasons. They read the Old Testament:

- to learn about things that happened in the past, especially events by which they believe God prepared the way for the coming of Jesus
- to learn about the writers' insights into what God is like and what he wants from those who believe in him
- to discover words used in the worship and praise of God and to make those words their own.

They read the New Testament:

- to learn about the life and teaching of Jesus
- to learn about the words and actions of the followers of Jesus.

Christians make a great deal of use of the Bible in both public and private **worship**.

Reading and preaching

Reading from the Bible is a central part of public worship. In many **services** one or more lessons are read to the whole **congregation**. The readings may be selected by the person leading the worship or they may be taken from a lectionary. (A lectionary is a book that gives lists of readings chosen so that virtually the whole Bible is covered over a period of time while appropriate passages are selected for special days and festivals.) Members of the congregation sometimes like to have a copy of the reading to help them concentrate on what is being read.

The readings are usually prepared carefully so that they can help the listeners to understand what is being read.

In many services one of the people leading the worship **preaches** a **sermon** (gives a message to the rest of the congregation). A sermon is often an explanation of the teaching of the Bible. The preacher explains how what is written in the Bible is relevant to everyday life.

Some Christians meet to study the Bible together in study groups. They choose a passage, then talk about its meaning and relevance to their lives. There are courses of study that they can use.

Individual Christians read the Bible as part of their private **prayer** and **meditation**. Many of them read a passage of the Bible every day, using lists of Bible readings, sometimes with notes to explain the meaning of the day's reading.

At the Eucharist

The part of the **Eucharist** during which the Bible is read and the sermon is preached is called the Liturgy of the Word. There are two or three readings from the Bible. The last reading is from one of the gospels.

The central act of the **rite** is based on the words of Jesus at the meal he shared with his disciples the night before he was crucified, the Last Supper.

> The Lord Jesus, on the night he was betrayed, took bread, and when he had given thanks, he broke it and said, 'This is my body, which is for you; do this in remembrance of me.' In the same way, after supper he took the cup, saying, 'This cup is the new covenant in my blood; do this, whenever you drink it, in remembrance of me.' (1 Corinthians 11: 23–5)

Prayers based on the Bible

Christians use prayers in their public and private worship. Sometimes prayers are taken from, or based on words in, the Bible. Compare the Lord's Prayer (page 54) with Luke 11: 2–4 and the Hail Mary (page 15) with Luke 1: 28, 42.

Hymns are worship songs and many are based on the Bible.

Bible passage	Hymn
At the name of Jesus every knee should bow, in heaven and on earth and under the earth, and every tongue confess that Jesus Christ is Lord, to the glory of God the Father. (Philippians 2: 10–11)	At the name of Jesus Every knee shall bow, Every tongue confess him King of glory now: 'Tis the Father's pleasure We should call him Lord, Who from the beginning Was the mighty Word.

The **Psalms** are ancient worship songs from the Old Testament. In Christian worship they are often sung or said in their original form. Many of them have been rewritten to be sung as hymns.

Here is a modern version of a psalm written about 3000 years ago. Compare it with an older version.

The Lord is my shepherd;
there is nothing I shall want.
Fresh and green are the pastures
where he gives me repose.
Near restful waters he leads me
to revive my drooping spirit.
He guides me along the right path;
he is true to his name.
If I should walk through the valley of darkness
no evil would I fear.
You are there with your crook and your staff;
with these you give me comfort.
(Psalm 23 © The Grail 1963)

Activities

1   Visit the website of the Bible Reading Fellowship (www.brf.org.uk). What can you find there about the way in which the organization helps people in their Bible reading? **IT 2.1, 2.2**

2   Ask members of the group in turn whether they own a Bible or if they know anyone who has one. If the answer is 'yes', consider these questions.
    a   How did you/that person get the Bible?
    b   Is that Bible special in any way?
    c   Was the Bible a gift? If so, why did the giver think it was suitable? **C 2.1a**

Key points

- Christians turn to the Bible so they can know and understand more about God and how human beings can come to know him better.
- Christians use the Bible in both their public and private worship.
- Much of Christian worship is based on the Bible.

The creeds

Key terms

Apostles' Creed a statement of belief based on the teaching of the apostles and containing the basic principles of the Christian faith

Church when written with a capital letter C, it refers to Christian people; it may mean a particular group of Christians or all Christians

Creed a statement of belief

Holy Spirit the third person of the Trinity; Christians believe the Holy Spirit is always with them, giving them strength and support

Trinity God the Father, God the Son and God the Holy Spirit – three persons but one God

A **creed** is a statement of belief. The word comes from the Latin word *credo*, meaning 'I believe'. The words 'I believe' are the opening words of the **Apostles' Creed** and the Nicene Creed, the two creeds most widely used by Christians.

The creeds are summaries of basic Christian beliefs, the foundations of the Christian faith. They are regularly recited in worship in some traditions.

The Nicene Creed

The Nicene Creed was written to define what Christians must believe. Those who did not accept the Nicene Creed were reckoned not to be true Christians. In particular, it spelt out what Christians should believe about Jesus Christ. It is important to believe that:

- there is only one God
- the Father, the Son and the **Holy Spirit** are each of them God – they are three distinct persons, but only one God
- Jesus Christ was completely God and at the same time completely human.

The Apostles' Creed

The Apostles' Creed was not written by the apostles. It was given this name because it sums up the most important teachings of the **apostles**.

It took shape over a long period of time. It was written to help people memorize the basic beliefs of Christianity.

- God the Father is the Creator.
- Jesus Christ, God the Son, was born of a virgin. He was crucified and rose again, and is now enthroned in heaven.
- The third person of the **Trinity** is the Holy Spirit.
- The **Church** is holy.
- For Christians there is the hope of forgiveness of sins and eternal life.

Belief is faith and trust

At a number of places in the creeds Christians say 'I believe in…' or 'We believe in…'. 'Believe in' is a strong statement. 'I believe in God' says much more than 'I believe that God exists.' It means 'I trust in God; I have faith in God.'

The Trinity

In the creeds Christians state their belief in the Trinity. This means that they believe in three persons who are together one God. The word 'Trinity' is not actually used. The creeds take it for granted that the Father, the Son and the Holy Spirit are each of them God. They are three distinct persons, but only one God.

People use examples such as these to help themselves understand the Trinity.

How are creeds used today?

Some traditions do not think creeds are necessary. For example, Baptists believe that the Bible is the only source of authority a Christian must accept. There is no higher authority. Other traditions give the creeds a much higher place.

- Roman Catholics accept the authority of the general councils of the Church. The Nicene Creed was approved at the Council of Nicaea (from which the creed gets its name) and at the Council of Constantinople, both in the fourth century.
- Roman Catholics also accept the whole body of the faithful, the Church as a whole, as a source of authority. The creeds contain the teachings accepted by the whole Church.
- Anglicans believe that the two creeds together make up one of the essentials of the Christian Church. (The others are the Bible, the sacraments of baptism and Holy Communion, and the orders of bishops, priests and deacons.)

Creeds are said or sung during worship in some traditions.

- This is a way of reminding worshippers of the main points of Christianity.
- The worshippers are declaring publicly that this is what they truly believe.
- The fact that the words are said by everyone together is a sign that they share these beliefs. The beliefs bind them together as a family.

Usually people stand to say the creed, as a sign of how important it is to believe in what they are saying. They may bow their heads when they say the name of Jesus.

Key points

- The creeds are statements of the main points of Christian belief.
- Some traditions regard the creeds as standards of what a person must believe to be a true Christian.
- In some traditions, the creeds are recited by the whole congregation, who stand as a sign of the importance of what they are saying.

The Apostles' Creed

I believe in God, the Father almighty,
creator of heaven and earth.

I believe in Jesus Christ, his only Son, our Lord,
who was conceived by the Holy Spirit,
born of the Virgin Mary,
suffered under Pontius Pilate,
was crucified, died, and was buried;
he descended to the dead.
On the third day he rose again;
he ascended into heaven;
he is seated at the right hand of the Father,
and he will come again to judge the living and
    the dead.

I believe in the Holy Spirit,
the holy catholic Church,
the communion of saints,
the forgiveness of sins,
the resurrection of the body,
and the life everlasting. Amen.

The Father

The Creed states the Christian belief in the Trinity. To begin, it talks about God the Father. It states that he is Almighty. There is no limit to his power. He is the creator of heaven and earth – in other words, of everything.

He did not just make heaven and earth. He gives life to heaven and earth, and all creatures who live in or on them. The Father continues to give life and power to the whole universe.

The Creed does not state how God created the universe. Christians are not bound to believe the version in Genesis.

The Son

The Creed speaks in detail of the Son. The life, death and **resurrection** of Jesus are the key to Christianity. The central events are stated simply.

Christians believe in Jesus as their Saviour. The Creed concentrates on who Jesus is and on the events by which Christians believe they can be saved.

The birth of Jesus

- Christians believe that Jesus is the Son of the Father. That does not mean that Jesus ever had a beginning – that there was a time when he did not exist. God the Son has always existed, with the Father and the Holy Spirit.

- The birth of Jesus is called the **incarnation**. It was different from the birth of any other human being. Before any of us was conceived, we did not exist as persons. Conception was when we began. With Jesus, Christians believe, it was different. He had always existed. He, the Son of God, then became a human being.

- In their gospels, both Matthew and Luke state that the birth of Jesus was unique. Mary did not have sexual intercourse with Joseph. It was the Holy Spirit who caused her to become pregnant. The child she was bearing was the Son of God.

The death of Jesus

- Christians believe that Jesus really did suffer and die. The **crucifixion** was an execution carried out under the authority of the Roman governor. To stress that it was a historical event, the governor is named – Pontius Pilate.

- Jesus' followers were so sure he was actually dead that they buried him.

For more information about the importance of the death of Jesus, see pages 104–5. The crucifixion and the resurrection are the **means of salvation**.

Jesus rose

- The resurrection is described simply as 'On the third day he rose again.'
- Jesus did not die again. His time on earth ended when he ascended to heaven.
- Jesus is not just someone who lived in the past. The Creed goes on to say where he is now – with the Father in glory.
- The Creed also looks to the future. Jesus will return to judge everyone – those who have died and those who are alive when he does return.

The Holy Spirit

Christians believe in the Holy Spirit as God, the third person of the Trinity. The belief is stated simply, without explanation. It is a central belief.

Christians believe that the Holy Spirit came to the Church at **Pentecost**, seven weeks after the resurrection of Jesus, and has been with Christians ever since. The Holy Spirit is present in the Church and in individual Christians. The Holy Spirit inspires people and guides them in what they say and do.

Belief in the presence of the Holy Spirit is of great importance to many Christians. Quakers wait on the Holy Spirit in their worship, believing that he may move them with a message for themselves and others at the meeting with them.

Charismatic worshippers believe that they are inspired by the Holy Spirit, both in their worship and in their everyday lives. Many Christians believe that the Holy Spirit is given in **baptism**, **confirmation** and **ordination**.

All Christians believe that the Holy Spirit is in no way limited to the Church or its ceremonies and worship. The Holy Spirit can inspire anyone at any stage in that person's life.

Other central beliefs

- Christians believe that the Church is not just a human organization. The Church was founded by Jesus. Through the Church all Christian people are united with Jesus himself and with each other – the Church is often called the **Body of Christ**. The Church is holy, which means it is dedicated to God and to serving him. The Church is catholic. The word 'catholic' means universal. It is important to Christians of all traditions that they belong to the one Church founded by Jesus Christ.
- 'The **communion of saints**' – 'communion' means being in fellowship together, 'saints' when used here means holy people. The bond that unites Christians is not limited to Christians alive now. Christians on earth and Christians in heaven are all members of God's family.
- Christians believe in forgiveness of **sins** because Jesus died to take away their sins. They do not expect every sin of every person to be forgiven. They believe that God will forgive those who are truly sorry and resolve not to sin again.
- When Christians say near the end of the creed that they believe in the resurrection of the body, they are not thinking of the resurrection of Jesus. They are thinking of their own future life. They do not mean that our physical bodies come to life again. They mean that there is a life after death that never ends. In that new life, individuals are in some way recognizable (see pages 108–9).

Activities

1 Many people believe that the universe is so wonderful that it cannot have happened by chance – there must be a creator. Do you think this is a reasonable opinion? Give reasons. **PS 2.1**

2 Imagine that someone accuses a child of doing something wrong. The child says to his or her mother, 'I didn't do it.' The mother might say, 'I believe my child.' Or she might say, 'I believe *in* my child.' Do both statements mean the same thing? **PS 2.1**

Key points

- The Apostles' Creed states a faith in God, Father, Son and Holy Spirit.
- Particular stress is placed on Jesus, Son of God, and his life, death and resurrection.
- The Creed includes, as matters of faith, belief in the Church, the communion of saints, forgiveness of sins and eternal life.

Mary, Mother of God

Mary has by grace been exalted above all angels and men to a place second only to her Son, as the most holy Mother of God who was involved in the mysteries of Christ.

(Catholic bishops at **Vatican II**)

Conceived by the Holy Spirit, born of the Virgin Mary

Catholics hold Mary in greater honour than any other human being. She was chosen to be the human mother of God the Son, Jesus Christ. Her son, Jesus, was divine – God the Son. He was also fully human, born of a human mother. The Christian faith depends on the belief that Jesus Christ, the Son of God, was born a human being.

'God sent his son, born of a woman.' (Galatians 4: 4) Mary was that woman, with a key role in God's plan for the salvation of the world.

Mary, mother of Jesus

Luke describes how Mary learned that she was to be the mother of the Messiah, the leader coming from God.

In the sixth month, God sent the angel Gabriel to Nazareth, a town in Galilee, to a virgin pledged to be married to a man named Joseph, a descendant of David. The virgin's name was Mary. The angel went to her and said, 'Greetings, you who are highly favoured! The Lord is with you.' Mary was greatly troubled at his words and wondered what kind of greeting this might be. But the angel said to her, 'Do not be afraid, Mary, you have found favour with God. You will be with child and give birth to a son, and you are to give him the name Jesus. He will be great and will be called the Son of the Most High.' 'How will this be,' Mary asked the angel, 'since I am a virgin?' The angel answered, 'The Holy Spirit will come upon you, and the power of the Most High will overshadow you. So the holy one to be born will be called the Son of God.' 'I am the Lord's servant,' Mary answered. 'May it be to me as you have said.' (Luke 1: 26–32, 34–5, 38)

It is almost impossible to imagine what Mary felt when she saw Gabriel. We have no idea how Gabriel appeared to her. What he said to her must have sounded quite incredible.

- 'You have found favour with God.' God had chosen her.
- She would have a child who would be called 'the Son of the Most High'.

This event is known as the **Annunciation**.

The Virgin Birth

In the passage from Luke's Gospel, Mary asked Gabriel, 'How will this be since I am a virgin?' Gabriel answered, 'The Holy Spirit will come upon you, and the power of the Most High will overshadow you. So the holy one to be born will be called the Son of God.'

In Matthew's Gospel, the same idea is presented from Joseph's side.

This is how the birth of Jesus Christ came about: His mother Mary was pledged to be married to Joseph, but before they came together, she was found to be with child through the Holy Spirit. Because Joseph her husband was a righteous man and did not want to expose her to public disgrace, he had in mind to divorce her quietly. But after he had considered this, an angel of the Lord appeared to him in a dream and said, 'Joseph, son of David, do not be afraid to take

Mary home as your wife, because what is conceived in her is from the Holy Spirit. She will give birth to a son, and you are to give him the name Jesus, because he will save his people from their sins.' When Joseph woke up, he did what the angel of the Lord had commanded and took Mary home as his wife. But he had no union with her until she gave birth to a son. And he gave him the name Jesus.
(Matthew 1: 18–21, 24–5)

The **doctrine** of the Virgin Birth is based on these narratives. The doctrine is that at the time when Mary conceived and then gave birth to Jesus, she was a virgin. The Holy Spirit caused her to conceive Jesus.

Mother of God

Mary's child was Jesus, God the Son, the second person of the Trinity. To be chosen to be the mother of the Son of God was an immense honour. Christians think of her bearing God's son in her womb. They imagine her feelings when the child was born and shepherds came, saying that they had been told by angels about the birth of the Saviour, Christ the Lord. Luke writes that when the shepherds went away, 'Mary treasured up all these things and pondered them in her heart.' (Luke 2: 19)

The gospels contain only one glimpse of the childhood of Jesus. Joseph and Mary took Jesus, when he was twelve, to the Passover celebration in Jerusalem. When they were ready to return home, Jesus could not be found. Eventually they found him in the Temple, amazing the gathered priests with his understanding and answers. Mary naturally said, 'Your father and I have been anxiously searching for you.' Jesus answered, 'Didn't you know I had to be in my Father's house?'

They took Jesus back to Nazareth, where he 'was obedient to them. But his mother treasured all these things in her heart.' (Luke 2: 41–52)

Christians often picture what life in the family home at Nazareth must have been like. In particular, they imagine a close, loving relationship between Jesus and Mary.

Activities

1   Look at the expression on the faces of Mary and Jesus in the photo above. Why has the artist shown them in this way?
    PS 2.1

2   In groups, discuss whether it is important for Christians to believe that Jesus grew up in a normal family.
    C 2.1, 2.2; PS 2.1; WO 2.1, 2.2

Key points

- Mary is honoured because she conceived and gave birth to Jesus, the Son of God, through the action of God the Holy Spirit.
- Mary is honoured as the Mother of God.

Mary's place in Roman Catholic belief

Mary's place in Catholic Devotion

Mary is honoured as the Mother of God, the human mother who gave birth to the Son of God. She is sometimes known by the title 'Theotokos', a Greek word meaning 'God-bearer'.

'Since the Son of God became incarnate and was born from her truly and properly, we confess her to be truly and properly the Mother of God.' (Pope John II, 534 AD)

Note the title *Mother of God* was not used originally to honour Mary, but to stress that Jesus, her child, is truly God the Son. Christians believe that Jesus is one being, truly God and truly human. If he was one being and Mary was his mother, then Mary is the mother of God.

Festivals of Mary

Two festivals in particular celebrate events relating to ways in which Mary is believed by many Catholics to be unique. One relates to the beginning and one to the end of Mary's life. Both beliefs have been declared to be **dogmas** of the Roman Catholic Church.

The feast of the Immaculate Conception

This is celebrated on 8 December. Note that the Immaculate Conception is *not* the same as the Virgin Birth. The Immaculate Conception occurred when Mary was conceived in the womb of her mother.

It was a natural human conception following intercourse between Mary's parents, Anne and Joachim. God caused Mary to be born free from original sin (see page 66), so that she would be a fit person to be the Mother of God.

Mary's birth is celebrated on 8 September.

The Feast of the Assumption

This is celebrated on 15 August. At the end of her life, Mary was received ('assumed') into heaven. There, eternally, she **intercedes** for the whole human family.

Mary and the Church

When Jesus ascended to heaven (see page 112), he left his followers to establish his Church. They went to Jerusalem to wait for the coming of the Holy Spirit. There were 120 of them. In Acts 1: 12–14, apart from the Apostles, only Mary is named as being among them.

Mary is human; in no way do Christians regard her as more than human. She is in heaven now because Jesus died and rose again. The bishops at Vatican II stated 'Mary is a member of the Church'. They did not issue a separate document about Mary at the end of the council. What they had to say about her was included in the document on the Church. But her unique role as the mother of Jesus gives her a unique relationship with the Church.

- Mary is the mother of all Christians because, by giving birth to Jesus, she made it possible for Christians to have new life in Jesus. Through the Church, Christians are born again in Baptism.
- Mary is pure and faithful, as the Church is called to be.
- Mary prays for the human race, as does the Church.
- Mary shares fully in the resurrection of Jesus, as the Church is destined to do.

Mary – Mediatrix

Catholics pray through Mary. They believe that she prays for them. She is the **Mediatrix** – a person who mediates, pleads to God for other people.

Catholics do not pray to Mary in the same way that they pray to God. They do not believe that she can answer prayer. They believe that she prays for them, intercedes for them.

Catholics are as familiar with the Hail Mary as they are with the Lord's Prayer.

Hail Mary, full of grace
the Lord is with you
Blessed are you among women,
and blessed is the fruit of your womb, Jesus.
Holy Mary, Mother of God,
pray for us sinners now and at the hour of our death.

- The prayer starts with Gabriel's greeting at the Annunciation, approaching Mary with reverence and honour.
- It addresses her as holy, blessed by God and dedicated to the service of God.
- It asks her to pray for the individual and for all sinners, both during their lives and when, at death, they need the mercy and forgiveness of God.

Mary – role model and guide

Catholics look to Mary as the supreme example of a life dedicated to Jesus. She is a role model and a guide to the way they should serve God.

- When Gabriel told Mary that she was to be the mother of the Messiah, she accepted willingly and joyfully. 'I am the Lord's servant. May it be to me as you have said.' (Luke 1: 38)
- Mary had complete faith in her son. Read about how, at a wedding, Jesus turned water into wine (John 2: 1–11). Note how Mary said to the servants, 'Do whatever he tells you.' She knew that Jesus could and would do what was needed.
- Mary is a model of faithfulness to God, even through pain. When she and Joseph took the infant Jesus to the temple in Jerusalem, it was prophesied 'A sword will pierce your own soul too'. The prophecy came true when Mary was at the foot of the cross watching Jesus die.

The Pietá – Mary holding the body of the crucified Jesus. The artist shows the anguish in the mother's face.

Activities

1 Compose a prayer that Catholics might use when asking Mary to intercede for them. In what way would that prayer differ from one addressed to God? **PS 2.1**

2 In what ways might belief in Mary as a role model affect a Catholic's way of life? **PS 2.1**

Key points

- Catholics believe that Mary was conceived free from original sin and that at the end of her life, she was taken bodily into heaven.
- Catholics believe that Mary has a unique place in the Church.
- They pray to Mary, asking her to intercede for them.
- They look up to her as a role model and a guide.

Exam tips and practice questions

Below are some sample exam questions on the Bible, the creeds and Mary. Questions **1** and **2** include examiner's tips to give you hints on how to score full marks. Questions **3** and **4** are for you to try on your own.

1   Different Christians mean different things when they say that the Bible is the Word of God. Explain two contrasting ways in which Christians understand the Bible to be the Word of God. *(8 marks)*

2   'I believe in God, but I don't believe that he created the universe.' Do you think a person who says this can be called a Christian? Give reasons for your answer, showing that you have considered more than one point of view. *(5 marks)*

Now try these questions with no hints. Before you write an answer, try to write down your own hints on how to score full marks.

3   What do Roman Catholics believe about Mary? Why is she important to them? *(6 marks)*

4   'The Bible is a source of comfort and encouragement to Christians.' Do you agree? Give reasons for your answer, showing that you have considered more than one point of view. *(5 marks)*

How to score full marks

The examiner would be marking on the basis of levels of response (see page vi), so make sure your responses are full and accurate.

1   This is a question to test what you know. The examiner expects you to select two from literalists, fundamentalists, conservatives and liberals. Make clear which groups you have chosen. Make sure you describe clearly what each group believes. If you are not sure of the answer, page 4 should help you.

2   This is an evaluation question to make you think and to test how well you can assess a problem or situation. Look for arguments **for** and **against** the statement you have to discuss.

No more than three marks would be given to a response that only looked at one side of the question. Note that you are not being asked if you think the account in Genesis, chapter 1 is true.

Note that in an exam you might simply be asked to give one or two examples of different ways in which Christians interpret the Bible. Make sure you describe each interpretation clearly and identify the groups from which they are taken (for example, fundamentalists and liberals) and describe each one clearly.

The Church and places of worship

This section includes:

- The Church – God's family
- The Pope
- The teaching authority of the Church
- The ministry
- Worship
- Introduction to church buildings
- Roman Catholic church buildings
- Anglican and Orthodox church buildings
- Pulpit-centred church buildings.

In this section you will learn about how Christians think of the Church as God's family – the Body of Christ. There are units on the roles of the Pope and the bishops as guardians of the authority of the church. The unit on the ministry looks at the vocations of all Christians and in particular of the ordained ministry and those in religious orders.

The section looks at worship, both liturgical and non-liturgical, both structured and spontaneous. It looks at places of worship from a number of traditions and examines the use made of them.

The Church – God's family

Different traditions – one faith.

If you walk through the centre of a town or city, you will probably pass a number of church buildings. They belong to different Christian traditions – Baptist, Church of England, Methodist, Orthodox, Quaker, Roman Catholic, Salvation Army, United Reformed Church and many more.

In the Apostles' Creed, Christians say they believe in 'the holy catholic Church'. This means they believe in the one Church founded by Jesus Christ.

To some Christians, the Church is much more than a human organization. It is inspired and guided by God the Holy Spirit.

The Church – the Body of Christ

One expression used by the apostle Paul in the New Testament to describe the Church is the 'Body of Christ'. This expression is understood in a number of ways.

- Where a person's body is, that person is present and can act. Read the following prayer of St Theresa of Avila – it is through the Church that the love of God can be shown to the world.

Christ has no body on earth but yours,
No hands but yours,
No feet but yours.
Yours are the eyes through which Christ's compassion is to look out on the world.
Yours are the feet with which he is to go about doing good.
Yours are the hands with which he is to bless mankind now.

- A body is made up of many parts. In the same way, the Church is made up of many parts – individual Christians and groups of Christians. Each person or group has something to contribute to the life of the whole Church.
- No part of the body is insignificant or unnecessary. All are of value for who they are.
- The whole body experiences joy or sorrow because the body is a unity. So, when one Christian or one part of the Church is suffering, everyone should feel for them. When one Christian has something to celebrate, everyone should rejoice with them.

Christians also speak of the consecrated bread at the Eucharist as the Body of Christ (see pages 44–5). In both cases, 'the Body of Christ' is a sign of Jesus being present with his followers and of them being bonded together with each other.

The Church – the family of God

Jesus taught his disciples to address God as 'Our Father'. It is therefore natural for Christians to think of the Church as a family. In a family there may be disagreements or tensions, but there is still a bond between its members. They share food together. In times of trouble, they turn to one another for support. The image of the family, like that of the Body of Christ, emphasizes the closeness Christians should feel with God and with each other. This closeness goes beyond local churches and communities. The Church includes all Christians throughout the world and in heaven as well.

The different traditions today

The differences that caused the divisions in the Church count for very little in the twenty-first century. For example, there are Christians still who see themselves as protesting against the Roman Catholic tradition, but they are very few and the word 'Protestant' is not used a great deal. Yet the different traditions continue.

- Christians have different beliefs. Sometimes these beliefs affect what they do. For example, many Christians believe that it is right to baptize infants. Others believe that baptism should wait until a person is able to make a conscious decision to be a Christian.
- Christians worship in different ways. This is seen as a positive thing. Some people feel more at home with one form of worship, others prefer to worship in another way. Different ways of worshipping help different people to be near to God.

Christians together

If the Church is the family of God, the Body of Christ, Christians should feel a strong sense of togetherness. This togetherness shows itself in different ways.

- Christians work together to help others – to show what Jesus called 'love for one's neighbour'. Sometimes Christians get together to help people in their area who are in need. Sometimes it is shown by Christians of different traditions joining to support an agency such as Christian Aid or Tearfund.

- People from different traditions meet from time to time to worship together, for example, during Christian Unity Week, January 18–25.
- Sometimes Christians join in acts of witness to show they are Christians and that there is a bond between them. An example is a procession through a town centre on **Good Friday**. Those walking in the procession show that they are followers of Jesus Christ, marking this holy day together.
- In some places different traditions share church buildings. Sometimes they worship together; sometimes they worship according to their different traditions.

The trend towards stronger links and greater co-operation among the Christian traditions is called the **Ecumenical** Movement.

Activities

1 Look around your neighbourhood or the nearest town centre. Note the different Christian places of worship that you see. What differences do you notice in the buildings themselves? Are there differences in what is shown on the noticeboards outside the buildings? Try to find out if the Christians who worship in these different places ever meet together or worship together. **PS 2.1**

2 Read what Paul wrote in 1 Corinthians 12: 12–31. Explain what he is saying about the Church as the Body of Christ. **PS 2.1, 2.3**

Key points

- Christians believe in the one Church founded by Jesus Christ.
- They use expressions such as the Body of Christ and the family of God to describe the Church.
- For various reasons there are different Christian traditions. In the twenty-first century, these traditions work closely together.

The Pope

Head of the Roman Catholic Church

The Pope is Bishop of Rome and head of the Roman Catholic Church. 'Pope' simply means 'father' and he is often addressed as 'The Holy Father.'

The Pope is elected to serve the Catholic Church for the remainder of his life. He is chosen by the '**Electoral College**', which is made up of all those bishops who have been given the special position of **Cardinal**. Each cardinal has the right to be elected as Pope. It is important to remember that each cardinal is a bishop, that each bishop is a priest and that each priest comes from an ordinary family. Therefore, the Pope is a representative of every member of the Church.

The Pope, as Bishop of Rome, is based in Rome, the capital of Italy. As he is the head of a world-wide Church, the Pope's official residence and all the central offices of the Roman Catholic Church are based in Vatican City. Although Vatican City is to be found in the centre of Rome, it is a city within a city. It is the world's smallest independent state and is represented at the United Nations.

St Peter's Basilica in Vatican City, built over the tomb of Peter, is the mother church of Roman Catholicism.

Roman Catholics, and many other Christians, do not look upon the Pope as just the head of the Roman Catholic Church. They believe that he has a unique role to play, both historically and spiritually, as a person with authority throughout the whole Christian Church. This role is two-fold – as 'successor to Peter' and as spiritual guide.

Successor to Peter

Many Christians look upon the apostle Peter as the first bishop of Rome. Therefore, Roman Catholics believe that all bishops of Roman down through history have been his successors. For Christians to say that the Pope is 'successor to Peter' means a great deal. It is important to look at the following:

1 The major role the apostle Peter seemed to play in the life of the early Church.
2 The position he held among the small group of original disciples who were chosen by Jesus to preach the gospel to all the nations of the world.

In the gospel accounts of the beginning of the Christian Church, Peter is given a central place.

● Jesus gave Peter authority over the community of Christians, saying 'You are Peter, and on this rock I will build my Church … I will give you the keys of the kingdom of Heaven.' (Matthew 16: 18–19)

- Before his crucifixion, Jesus gave Peter the responsibility of strengthening Jesus' followers in the troubles which lay ahead. He said, 'I have prayed for you, Simon, that your faith may not fail … strengthen your brothers.' (Luke 22: 32)
- After the resurrection, Jesus spoke to Peter about his future in the role of the Church, saying, 'Simon, son of John, do you truly love me? … Feed my sheep.' (John 21: 15–17)

The Pope is also known by the titles 'Supreme Pontiff of the universal Church', 'Sovereign of the State of Vatican City' and 'Vicar of Jesus Christ'. The importance of the Pope's role in the modern Church is to symbolize and bring about the unity of the whole Church. His is a role of service to his 'flock' and to the spreading of the gospel to the world. The Pope is sometimes described as 'the servant of the servants of God'.

Spiritual guide

Perhaps the most important way of describing the Pope's ministry is that it is a pastoral ministry. All bishops are looked upon as pastors and the Pope is often called the 'Supreme Pastor'. The word 'pastor' means 'shepherd'. According to the Bible, a shepherd is someone who cares for his flock, guides them down the right path, leads them to new pastures and protects them from evil. This is the responsibility of the 'successor of Peter', a duty that is shared by the bishops of the Church.

A major part of the Pope's role is to oversee the teaching of the Church in matters of faith and morals. Christians believe that the world-wide Church has a duty to proclaim the gospel of Jesus faithfully and to be a living example of the gospel in action. The Pope, as leader of the Roman Catholic Church, has special authority to make sure that Jesus' teachings are protected.

It is believed that the Holy Spirit has been given to the Church by God as a guide to all truth. Therefore, the Holy Spirit is said to protect the Church, especially the Pope, from error when solemn statements are made on topics of faith or morals. This is called **infallibility**, which literally means 'freedom from error'. The phrase **ex cathedra**, meaning 'from the throne', is used when the Pope gives a pronouncement on a teaching of

the Church with the full weight of his authority as leader of the Roman Catholic Church. Such pronouncements are considered by Roman Catholics to be **infallible**. However, in practice, popes rarely use their authority in this way.

When the Pope gives guidance to the Church, he may do so by issuing an **encyclical**. This is a statement given to all Catholics, often in the form of a letter. It is not thought to be infallible, but it does have the authority of the Pope's position in the Church. An example of an encyclical issued by Pope John Paul II is 'Ut Unum Sint', meaning 'That They May Be One'. In this encyclical, the Pope spoke of strengthening relations between the Roman Catholic Church and other Christian traditions.

Activities

1 Visit a website that offers more information on the Pope and the Vatican, for example, www.vatican.va/phome_en.htm. IT 2.1

2 In groups, find out the range of the Pope's authority throughout the world. Design a display showing the major groups of Roman Catholics across the world.
C 2.1, 2.2; PS 2.1, 2.2; WO 2.1, 2.2

Key points

- The Pope is the head of the Roman Catholic Church. As Bishop of Rome, he is seen as 'Successor to Peter'.
- The Pope is chosen by the Electoral College, the Cardinals of the Roman Catholic Church.
- He is seen as the 'Supreme Pastor', or shepherd, of all Roman Catholics.
- The Pope has special authority to ensure that Jesus' teachings are protected.
- The Holy Spirit is thought to protect the Pope from error when he makes formal statements about faith or morals. Roman Catholics believe that, at such times, his statements are infallible.

The teaching authority of the Church

What is authority?

Authority does not mean control or force. It is an influence resulting from knowledge. The teaching authority of the Church is not based on power or command, but on knowledge and understanding, which are believed to be gifts of the Holy Spirit.

From a Christian point of view, all authority comes from God. Christians believe that Jesus, as God the Son, taught with authority: 'The people were amazed at his teaching, because he taught as one who had authority' (Mark 1: 22). His authority was particularly obvious when he spoke of the kingdom of God, its nature and its demands. The teaching authority of the Church was first given to the apostles of Jesus. Theirs was a mission to continue Jesus' work of teaching about the kingdom of God.

> Therefore go and make disciples of all nations, baptizing them in the name of the Father and of the Son and of the Holy Spirit, and teaching them to obey everything I have commanded you. (Matthew 28: 19–20)

The over-riding tone of Jesus' ministry was one of service. He did not come to achieve power and control for himself, but to serve. Jesus exercised his authority in the manner of a servant – 'I am among you as one who serves' (Luke 22: 27). He expected his apostles to follow his example.

Teaching became an essential means of passing on the Christian faith once the first generation of apostles had died. Since that time, the teaching authority of the Church has been based on its primary task of proclaiming the gospel and building up and supporting the Church, the Body of Christ.

The Church's magisterium

The Latin word **magisterium** means 'teaching authority'. The word was formally adopted at the time of Vatican I (1869–70) to mean the teaching authority of the Church. As the Church is the whole people of God, the authority to teach is given to the Christian community as a whole. It is the responsibility of all Christians to teach the gospel of Christ as members of 'One, Holy, Catholic and Apostolic Church' (the Nicene Creed).

In practice, however, authority can only be exercised by certain people for the good of everyone. From the earliest days of Christianity, the teaching authority of the Church was placed in the hands of bishops. Many Christians believe that bishops are the successors in an unbroken line to the apostles of Jesus Christ. This is known as the **Apostolic Succession**.

The authority of the Pope and bishops

Supreme authority in the Roman Catholic Church is given to the whole college of bishops, led by the Pope. Theirs is a pastoral ministry, caring for their communities and leading them down the right paths of faith and morals. They also have an apostolic ministry, the bishops 'receive from the Lord the mission to teach all nations and to preach the Gospel to every creature' (Vatican II).

The Roman Catholic Church is both local and world-wide. Each bishop exercises his pastoral and apostolic ministry in a diocese. This contains many parishes and, in England, can cover two to three counties. Dioceses are grouped into provinces so that pastoral policies are consistent over a wide area and bishops can support each other in their work under the leadership of an archbishop. The provinces of a particular country can form themselves into a bishops' conference. There is, for example, a bishops' conference for England and Wales. There is also a European bishops' conference.

The Pope is also a diocesan bishop. But he is first and foremost pastor of the universal Church. This does not mean that he is the sole ruler of the Church. He shares the teaching authority of the Church, the magisterium, with the bishops throughout the world.

Guidance of the Holy Spirit

It is the responsibility of the Pope and the bishops to ensure that the teachings of Jesus are protected. They also have the authority to make decisions and statements concerning faith and morals for the Roman Catholic community. Roman Catholics believe that the Pope and the bishops are guided in their decision making and teaching by the Holy Spirit, who prevents them from falling into error.

This belief has its foundation in the New Testament. At the Last Supper, Jesus said to his apostles, 'The Holy Spirit, whom the Father will send in my name, will teach you all things and will remind you of everything I have said to you' (John 14: 26). He also said, 'When the Spirit of truth comes he will guide you into all truth' (John 16: 13). The twelve apostles were chosen by Jesus to have authority over the early Church in the same way as a shepherd guides and cares for his sheep. Modern bishops have the same responsibility in their role as direct successors to the first apostles.

General Councils of the Church

The term 'magisterium' may be used in two ways.

1 'Ordinary Magisterium' is the day-to-day teaching of the bishops and priests in their dioceses and, to a large extent, the Pope's teaching to the world-wide Church.
2 'Solemn Magisterium' is the teaching authority that is exercised only rarely by formal statements made by councils or the Pope himself. A solemn judgement or definition is given concerning an issue of faith or morals.

The Pope has the authority to call a general council of all the bishops of the Roman Catholic Church. The last three councils have been:

- Council of Trent (1545–63)
- First Vatican Council (Vatican I, 1869–70)
- Second Vatican Council (Vatican II, 1962–5).

Statements issued by these councils have the highest authority and they are guided by the Holy Spirit and should be embraced by the universal Church.

The Pope shares the magistereum with the bishops of the Church.

Activities

'There can be no proper leadership without respect and love.' Discuss in groups whether this statement is true. How far should it be true in:

- a family
- a school
- a country
- the Church? **C 2.1; WO 2.1**

Key points

- The teaching authority of the Roman Catholic Church is known as 'magisterium'.
- Christians believe that Jesus gave authority to his disciples to preach the gospel. Their teaching would be guided by the Spirit.
- Throughout the history of the Christian Church, bishops, including the Bishop of Rome, have traced their authority back in an unbroken line to the first apostles.
- Roman Catholics believe that the magisterium is protected from error by the continued work of the Holy Spirit.

The ministry

Key terms

Lay people Christians who are not ordained ministers

Ministry spiritual leadership

Ordained when someone is given authority for a particular role within the Church through laying on of hands by a bishop or other senior minister

Vocation

The word **vocation** means 'calling'. People who have vocations believe that God is calling them to a particular way of life.

Christians believe that anyone can have a vocation. If God is calling someone to be a Christian shopkeeper, taxi driver, hairdresser or factory worker, then that is their vocation, to be lived out in a Christian way. The word 'vocation' is most often used for occupations that involve serving and helping other people, such as doctors, nurses, teachers and missionaries. Priests and ministers believe they have vocations, as do monks and nuns and others who are trained to work in the service of the Church.

Every Christian has a ministry

Every Christian has a part in the Christian **ministry**. Jesus told his followers to tell other people about him. Paul called the Church the Body of Christ, with each person having a role.

Lay people are not **ordained**. However, they still have key roles in the life of the Church. They visit sick and housebound people. They lead Bible study groups and help to teach the younger Church members. Above all, they are Christians wherever they are and whatever they are doing. For instance, Christians who are mechanics or shop assistants show their faith simply by doing their jobs in a Christian spirit. Christians believe that they may be called by God to serve in particular ways.

The ordained ministry

There have always been leaders in the Church.

- Jesus chose twelve disciples to be with him and to be prepared to continue his work. They became apostles, sent out to spread the gospel.
- As the apostles and others preached, people were converted and became members of the Church. Groups of Christians formed in many places. They needed leaders to guide them and to lead their worship when the apostles moved on. Those leaders were known as episcopoi, the first bishops.

Bishops, priests and deacons

In the Roman Catholic tradition there are three orders, or levels, of ordained ministry. Each of these orders has authority for certain activities within the Church. This authority has been passed down from the apostles themselves and so those who are ordained to these orders are said to be in the Apostolic Succession. A bishop laying his hands on them ordains them, as the apostles did when they appointed others as ministers.

- A person is first made a **deacon**. A deacon can lead worship, preach, take funerals, baptize and marry people. For most people, being a deacon is a first step towards being a priest.
- The next order is **priest**. A priest can celebrate the Eucharist, which a deacon cannot do. A priest can give a blessing and can absolve people from their sins in God's name.
- The most senior order is **bishop**. He normally leads a confirmation service (see pages 72–3) and ordains deacons and priests. Bishops become bishops through the laying on of hands by other bishops.

Among Roman Catholics, only men may be ordained. The priest represents Jesus Christ, who was male himself and chose only males to be his apostles.

Positions which bishops, priests and deacons can hold for a time are, for example, archbishop or parish priest. They leave these positions when they move to other positions or retire. They remain bishops, priests and deacons forever.

Celibacy

Priests commit themselves to celibacy, that is, they promise never to marry or to have sexual intercourse. A priest must be fully available for whatever he is called to do without ties of the family to restrict him. He must be ready at any time to move to any place without needing to worry about, for example, his children's education. He is married to his parish or to other people in his care.

Bishops and priests have special responsibilities in the Church community.

- They have a special role in leading worship, particularly the Eucharist.
- They are close to people to support and guide them at crucial times in their lives. It is a great privilege to prepare people for marriage and to share with them the precious moment when they become husband and wife. It is also their responsibility to conduct in a dignified way the funeral of someone who has died and to support and comfort the close family.
- They have a special duty to teach and preach.
- They have pastoral duties. They visit and offer guidance to people facing problems or crises. They visit people who are ill and unable to come to places of worship.
- They liaise with leaders from other Christian traditions and with other groups in the local community.
- They have a duty to pray for the people who are members of the congregation.

Religious orders

Religious orders, for men or women, are either contemplative or active in the world. Contemplative orders, such as the Cistercians (male) and Carmelites and Poor Clares (female), dedicate themselves to lives of silence, solitude and prayer within their monasteries or convents. The Carmelites state on their website:

> The sisters value the companionship of Jesus above everything else. They are aware of sin and suffering, sadness and death throughout the world, and know that only Jesus has the answer. They are prepared to stake their lives on this. Their life's purpose is to love, and to bring all humanity closer to the Love of God.

Active orders, such as the Hospitaller Order of St John of God (male) and the Sisters of Mercy live lives of prayer, but are also active in the community, especially in teaching and caring for the sick.

Members of some religious orders take vows of poverty, chastity and obedience.

Priests and ministers can easily be recognized by the special clothes they wear.

Activities

1 Thought-tracking. Students choose different occupations. They talk/think about the ways in which the occupations chosen by themselves and by others can be regarded as vocations. **C 2.1a; WO 2.1, 2.2**

2 Visit the website of a contemplative order, for example, www.carmelnuns.org.uk, and of an active order, for example, www.hospitaller.co.uk. What sorts of lives do members of these orders lead? What do the sites tell you about the meaning of vocation? **PS 2.1; WO 2.1, 2.2**

Key points

- Roman Catholics believe that all Christians are called to some form of ministry or vocation.
- They believe in the Apostolic Succession of deacons, priests and bishops.
- Members of religious orders dedicate their lives to either contemplative or active service.

Worship

Key terms

Liturgical worship worship that follows a widely accepted set order of words and actions

Non-liturgical worship worship that does not follow a widely accepted set order of words and actions

Worth-ship

Worship means, in terms of the origin of the word, 'worth-ship'. It is about what something is worth and how precious it is.

To Christians, the idea of the worship of God is a very positive thing. Worship is about how much God means to Christians. They believe that God is almighty and is to be praised and adored. He is loving and Christians should respond to His love by loving Him – and loving one's neighbour.

There are many aspects to worship, as there are to prayer. Worship can be public, involving many fellow-worshippers. An act of public worship is often called a service. Worship can also be private, with someone praying to God in a quiet place, alone and undisturbed.

Liturgical worship

Liturgical worship follows a fixed written pattern. You will study examples of liturgical worship on pages 46–9, which describe the way in which the Eucharist is celebrated in many traditions.

As people arrive for the service, they are given books that contain the rite used week by week. The Bible readings and some of the prayers change to fit the theme for the Sunday or festival. The basic pattern stays the same.

A Roman Catholic from Britain attending Mass in any country of the world would be able to follow the service even without a book and without knowing a word of the language. The shape of the service and the actions would be very similar.

Many people enjoy liturgical worship because it is structured and familiar. They are using forms of service that have been used for centuries and in many places.

They feel they are sharing in worship with fellow-Christians in every part of the world. They sense a richness in the thought and language of the rite. The actions are full of meaning, especially those that echo the actions of Jesus himself at the Last Supper.

Non-liturgical worship

Non-liturgical worship does not rely on books or set forms of service. People leading the worship plan the service according to the particular congregation. The worship may well be structured. Such worship is usually Bible-centred. An example is the form of service that is frequently used in the Methodist, United Reformed and Baptist Churches (see pages 34–5).

Unstructured worship

Sometimes the worship is much less planned.

- There is a great sense of the Holy Spirit at work.
- There may be a general shape to the worship, with music, readings, preaching and prayers, but the atmosphere is free and relaxed.
- There are plenty of lively hymns, songs and choruses. At some points the worshippers are free to join in and contribute as they wish.
- There is a feeling of freedom and emotion about the worship. Worshippers may show their feelings by waving their arms in the air or calling out 'Alleluia' or 'Praise the Lord'.
- Anyone may lead the congregation in **extempore prayer** or may give a message to the whole gathering.
- Everything feels spontaneous and full of life.

This sort of worship is often called 'charismatic'. It is found in most Christian traditions. In particular, members of the Pioneer and Restoration Churches and of the Pentecostal movement, including the Elim Pentecostal Church and the Assemblies of God, worship regularly in this way.

One main feature of this worship is that Bible reading and study is very important. The preaching at Spring Harvest, a gathering of (mainly young) Christian people, is very Bible-centred and those who come to Spring Harvest do so expecting their faith to be built up by the preachers as well as by the powerful experience of charismatic worship. At their meetings, Quakers wait for the Holy Spirit to guide them in what they should say. Their meetings are completely unstructured. In the same way, the worship in house churches can be very free and flexible.

Extempore prayer

Extempore prayer comes from the thoughts and feelings of the person speaking. People praying extempore simply use their own words as they pray. Extempore prayer is spontaneous and comes from the heart. Extempore prayer is an important part of non-liturgical worship, especially when it is less structured. It is also used in liturgical worship, especially for **intercession**.

Extempore prayer can be anything, depending on the person who is praying. A typical example might be something like this:

> O God, I just thank you for everything. The world is so wonderful and I am so happy. And, God, I want to thank you more than anything, God, for Jesus. I know there are lots of people who are suffering. O God, please help these poor people and may their suffering be over. I know you can do it, God. Please do help them. Oh Jesus, I do love you. Amen.

Activities

1 Using the Internet, type 'Pentecostal' into a search engine and visit the websites of some of the Pentecostal churches listed. What can you discover about the way in which they worship? If you prefer, visit the website of Spring Harvest (www.springh.org). For whom is Spring Harvest intended? What are the organization's aims and how does it work to achieve those aims? **IT 2.1, 2.2**

2 Working in groups, imagine that you are a Church youth group that is going to lead the worship for the whole congregation one Sunday. Plan together the form that the worship should take and give reasons why you have chosen that particular form. Compare what you have planned with the other groups. **PS 2.1, 2.2, WO 2.1, 2.2, 2.3**

Key points

- Liturgical worship follows a fixed, familiar pattern.
- Non-liturgical worship may be structured or unstructured.
- Charismatic worship is noted for being free and lively.
- Extempore prayer is spontaneous, composed on the spot by the person leading the prayer.

Young Christians join in the lively charismatic worship of Spring Harvest.

Introduction to church buildings

Key terms

church when written with a small letter c, it refers to a place where Christians worship

Places for worship

Many Christians speak of their place of worship as the house of God, the place where the family of God meet to worship and for such important events as baptisms, weddings and funerals. It is also a place of quiet reflection and prayer.

A **church** building is like any other building in two important ways:

- It is designed for a purpose – in the case of a church building, the purpose is worship.
- It has a distinctive atmosphere – the architect should design the building so as to create the right feeling.

As you visit church buildings, you will notice differences between them. Often the differences are because the buildings are used in different ways.

- Some buildings are altar-centred. The main actions in the worship take place at or near the altar. In these churches, the Eucharist is the main act of worship.
- Some buildings are **pulpit**-centred. In these churches the main act of worship is based on reading the Bible and preaching.

You will notice differences between the feeling you get in some church buildings and the feeling you get in others. Some buildings are light, and it is easy to relax in them and feel at home. Others fill a person with awe and wonder.

Another thing you may notice in some churches is the range of ornaments and symbols. You may see crosses and crucifixes, icons and stained glass windows, statues and **stations of the cross** (pictures or other symbols of the places along the route Jesus took as he went to his crucifixion – see page 60). These symbols are used as aids to worship, objects that help worshippers to fix their thoughts on prayer. Some buildings have none of these objects since they are regarded as unnecessary distractions.

The focal point

It is important to understand what is meant by the focal point of any room or meeting place. The structure of a room or building is often designed in such a way that attention is immediately drawn to one point. The main room in your home may have a focal point, possibly the television or the fireplace. Your classroom has a focal point – what is it?

Every place of worship needs a focal point. This is where the main action of the service takes place. The focal point is almost always one of two pieces of furniture:

- the altar or communion table
- the pulpit.

An altar-centred church in which the main act of worship is the Eucharist.

28

In this pulpit-centred church, the main emphasis in worship is on reading and preaching the word of God.

The exterior of church buildings

Of all buildings in any town or village, churches are among the most distinctive. Some churches have towers, others have steeples. The tower or steeple can be seen from some distance away, unless modern higher buildings have obscured them from view. Many towers have bells that are rung to call people to worship.

The height of many churches makes them more impressive. Many also have crosses or other Christian symbols to mark them out as Christian places of worship.

Some churches have churchyards round them – burial places for members of the community. A traditional name for a churchyard is 'God's acre'.

Steeples, symbolically pointing to heaven, are a familiar sight.

Activities

1   Look at the photo of the village church above. Would it matter if the steeple were removed? To whom would it matter and why? **PS 2.1**
2   In small groups, compare the feeling of walking into a school hall with the feeling of walking into a church building. Each group should write down its views and report back to the whole class.
    C 2.1a, 2.1b, WO 2.1, 2.2

Key points

- Church buildings are designed for a purpose – the worship of God.
- Each church building has a distinctive atmosphere. It may inspire people to awe or it may make them feel relaxed.
- Some church buildings contain many symbols and holy objects.

Steeple   Tower

Some churches have towers, others have steeples.

Roman Catholic Church buildings

Key terms

Sacrament a symbol or sign through which Christians receive strength and guidance from God to help them in their everyday lives. Baptism and Eucharist are regarded as the most important of the sacraments, being based on the commands of Jesus to go and baptize people of all nations and to receive the bread and wine in remembrance of him.

The words 'receiving the sacrament' are often used to mean receiving the consecrated bread and wine, the Body and Blood of Christ.

Catholic worship

The main action of the Mass takes place at the altar, where the priest consecrates bread and wine. Therefore, a Roman Catholic Church building is altar-centred. The design of the building must focus on the altar. The altar stands in the sanctuary, which is usually raised so that everyone present can see what is happening. There are usually candles on the altar. Above the sanctuary hangs a crucifix.

The word 'altar' reminds Christians of the sacrifices and death of Jesus on the cross. In the Old Testament, altars were used to offer sacrifices of praise and repentance to God. Christians believe that Jesus made the ultimate sacrifice of himself for the sake of all people. The altar is also a table. Communicants are sharing a **fellowship meal**, as they remember the meal Jesus shared with his disciples at the Last Supper. Christians believe that Jesus is present with his followers when they celebrate Holy Communion together.

The altar may be covered with a coloured cloth, called a frontal. The colour of the frontal changes with the different seasons of the Christian year. For example, white or gold is used at the joyful festivals of Christmas, Epiphany, Easter and Ascension. Purple is used during Advent and Lent, the solemn times of preparation for the great festivals of Christmas and Easter.

Near the altar is the lectern or reading desk used for the Liturgy of the Word and the chair from which the service is led. The chair is an important symbol of the authority of Christ and the principle celebrant will often speak or preach from the chair rather than from the lectern. In modern Roman Catholic churches, all the seating is arranged as close to the sanctuary as possible, often on three sides, with the sanctuary at the centre. Older churches were designed for a different style of worship and nowadays their layout is often modified to suit modern needs.

Tabernacle

A tabernacle is a safe-like place in which consecrated bread and wine are kept. It may be freestanding, perhaps on a ledge behind the altar, or be built into the wall near or behind the altar. There is a light by the tabernacle that remains lit as a sign that the **sacrament** is present.

The sacrament that is kept (the correct term is 'reserved') there is for those who are unable to come to church and who receive the sacrament from the priest in their own homes. It is also a sign of the continuing presence of Jesus with his Church and is therefore, a focus for prayer and devotion. Often Roman Catholics, on entering a church, go down on one knee ('genuflect') towards the tabernacle in honour of the presence of Jesus in the sacrament.

Confessionals

A confessional may consist of two small rooms, with a grill or curtain between them. This is for the sacrament of reconciliation, also known as confession. The priest sits in one room and the person confessing sins (the penitent) kneels in the other. Very often nowadays, priest and penitent sit together in a small room. When penitents have confessed their sins, the priest gives them a small task (a **penance**), such as a reading from the Bible or a prayer, and then **absolves** them (tells them their sins are forgiven).

The Church and places of worship

Baptistry

This is a small area set aside for the sacrament of baptism. Its main feature is the font. It is more usual nowadays for the baptistry to be at the front of the congregation, or to be moveable, rather than by the main door. It is important for the congregation to be able to see the action of the service and to welcome the new member of the Church.

Other features

As people come into the church they pass a holy water stoup or small font, containing holy water, blessed in the same way as water for baptism. They sign themselves with the water as they enter the church to remind themselves of their own baptism. Other important features of a Roman Catholic Church are Stations of the Cross and statues with **votive candles** to symbolize the prayers that are offered.

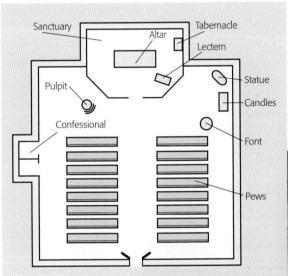

Activities

1 Visit a parish website. What can you discover here about Roman Catholic Church buildings and the way they are used? Sites you can visit include:
   - www.sacredheartblackburn.org.uk/frames.htm
   - www.marek.clara.net/ **IT 2.1, 2.2**

2 Why is it important that an architect designing a church building makes sure that everyone can see and hear? **PS 2.1**

Key points

- The focal point of a Roman Catholic Church building is the altar, the place at which the main action of the Mass takes place.
- Other distinctive features of the building are the lectern, the chair, the crucifix, the font, the tabernacle and the confessional.
- Stations of the Cross and statues are there as aids to prayer.

Inside a Roman Catholic church.

Anglican and Orthodox church buildings

Anglican

Anglicans are those Christians who are in communion with the Archbishop of Canterbury. There are Anglicans in many parts of the world. Anglicans have an ordained **episcopal** ministry.

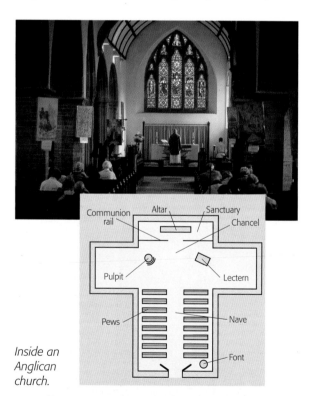

Inside an Anglican church.

The main act of worship

The main act of worship is the Eucharist. The main action of the Eucharist takes place at the altar. Therefore, the church building is altar-centred.

The congregation sit in the nave. In some churches there are areas to the sides of the nave called the aisles. The area around the altar is called the sanctuary. The area between the nave and the sanctuary, in which the choir may sit, is the chancel.

The central action in the service is the consecration of the bread and wine to be the Body and Blood of Jesus Christ. After the consecration, the congregation come to receive Holy Communion. They usually kneel at the communion rail, which divides the sanctuary from the chancel.

The altar is given a central, prominent place so that everyone can see and hear the priest and to emphasize the importance of what happens there.

The action of the Eucharist influences the design of the building in other ways.

- Readings from the Bible are read from the lectern. The sermon is preached either from the lectern or the pulpit. The pulpit is a raised structure for preaching. It is raised so that the preacher can be seen and heard. It is important that the reader or preacher can be seen and heard in all parts of the building, so the lectern and the pulpit have to be prominent.
- The congregation must be able to come to receive communion by a simple route.

Baptism

Infant baptism is the usual practice in the Anglican Church. Adults and older children are also baptized. Baptism takes place at the font, traditionally placed near the door, symbolizing baptism as an entrance to the church, but sometimes in front of the congregation, so that all may witness more easily the welcome of a new member into the church.

Other features

Most Anglican churches have an organ and a choir, for whom there is a special seating area.

In older buildings, you may find the Lord's Prayer and Ten Commandments on the walls. In times when books were rare and expensive, this was a way of making them accessible to people who could read.

In some larger buildings you will find a lady chapel and other side chapels.

Orthodox

The Orthodox Churches have their roots in countries in Eastern Europe and Asia, among them Greece, Russia and Armenia. They accept the authority of the Bible and of the creeds. Their ministry is episcopal.

The main feature of the church building is the **iconostasis**, a screen that goes across the entire width of the church. On one side are the people sharing in the worship, men and women sitting or standing separately from each other. On the other side is the sanctuary. The screen represents the division between earth and heaven.

The sanctuary is seen to be particularly holy. Only the priest and his assistant can enter it. The priest leads the worship from the sanctuary and the people respond. The altar is in the sanctuary and it is here that the bread and wine are consecrated to be the Body and Blood of Jesus during the **Divine Liturgy** (see page 48).

In the centre of the iconostasis are the Royal Doors, behind which there is a curtain. The doors remain closed and the curtain drawn for most of the service but there are points when the priest comes through them bringing heaven closer to earth.

- The Lesser Entrance. The book of the Gospel is carried through the Royal Doors by the priest. This is the Word of God brought to the people.
- The Greater Entrance. The offerings of the people, the bread and the wine, together with the offering of money, are taken through the Royal Doors. The priest lays the gifts on the altar.
- After the consecration, the bread and wine are brought out and given to the people.

Icons

The iconostasis is covered with **icons**. It is believed that icons are more than religious pictures. They are channels of God's grace, there is a spiritual power in them as they contain something of the spirit of the person portrayed. Throughout the **Liturgy**, the people, who cannot see the priest in the sanctuary, are able to focus their attention on the iconostasis and, in particular, the icons.

An icon is placed at the main entrance of the church. People kiss the icon as they enter, signing themselves with the cross as they do so.

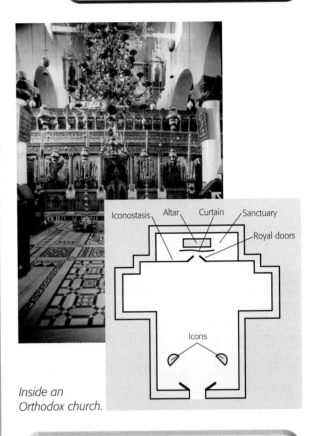

Inside an Orthodox church.

Activities

1 Forum theatre. Two students take the roles of Anglican and Roman Catholic church members. They are discussing the sharing of a church building, which they are planning together. **C 2.1a; PS 2.2, 2.3; WO 2.2, 2.3**

2 In an Orthodox Church there is an area (the sanctuary), which the ordinary worshipper may not enter. Discuss whether having such an area in the church creates a different atmosphere. If there is a difference, what is it and why? **C 2.1a; WO 2.1, 2.2**

Key points

- Both Orthodox and Anglican churches are altar-centred.
- The pulpit and lectern are also prominent in an Anglican church.
- The distinctive feature of an Orthodox church is the iconostasis.

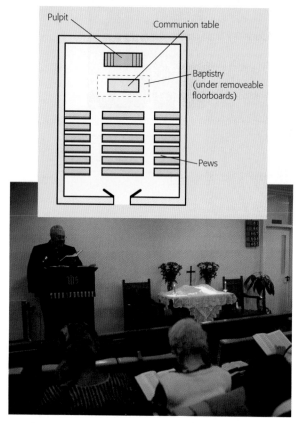

A pulpit-centred church building. In a Baptist church, the baptistry will often be under the communion table.

The main act of worship

The main act of worship in most Methodist, United Reformed and Baptist churches is based on the Bible. Lessons are read and the sermon is preached. For that reason the pulpit is the central piece of furniture, the focal point.

The worship will often follow a pattern. Here is an outline of a typical Sunday service.

- A hymn of praise sets the tone of the service, turning the thoughts of the people to God.
- The minister leads the congregation in prayer, focusing on the praise of God. The congregation join in the Lord's Prayer.
- Two Bible lessons are read.
- There are prayers of intercession.
- The organ plays quietly while the congregation's gifts of money are received. A hymn is sung.
- The preacher preaches the sermon.

- After the sermon, the congregation sing a final hymn. The service ends with a blessing.

Other worship

Holy Communion is celebrated once or twice a month in these traditions. The communion table has a central position, in front of or alongside the pulpit. It is called a table because these traditions stress the idea of communion as a shared meal, bonding them with fellow Christians and with Jesus himself.

The church buildings of these traditions look very similar. One significant difference arises from different beliefs concerning baptism. Baptists baptize by total immersion (see pages 70–1). A baptistry is needed, a small pool covered by floorboards except when needed for baptism. In the Methodist and United Reformed Churches, baptism is by pouring water on the forehead of the candidate, who may be an infant. This takes place at the font.

Symbols or ornaments are few in these church buildings. The most likely symbol is a plain cross.

The Quakers

A Quaker meeting house

Quakers (also known as the Religious Society of Friends) believe that in each human there is an inner light, a part of God's own Spirit. They believe very strongly that God reveals the truth to people in the present day, just as much as any other time. A Quaker meeting is quite different from acts of worship in other places. Those attending the meeting sit in silence around a central table. The Quakers are waiting on the Holy Spirit.

When Quakers meet for worship, they sit in such a way, in a circle or square, that they are conscious of each other. They sit in silence and the silence becomes more than a lack of sound. In fact, the sounds they hear, people talking in the street outside or the noise of a motorbike, become part of their consciousness. They share the experience of silence because they are worshipping together.

There is no minister to lead the worship. Quakers believe that the Spirit may move one or more of them to speak during a meeting.

Seats

Table

A Quaker meeting.

It does not matter who speaks. It may be someone old or young, someone who has been a Friend for many years or a first time visitor. What is said depends on the speaker. One person may read from the scriptures or may talk about the life and teaching of Jesus. They may talk about their own lives and the place of their faith in their everyday lives. Sometimes no one speaks at all during a meeting.

When someone has spoken, it is very rare that someone else answers or comments on what has been said. Everyone will listen to what has been said. Some will find in it a message from God. Others will reflect on it to see if it has a special relevance for them. Others may think for a short time, then return to what they had been thinking before the other Friend spoke. At the end, a handshake is passed round.

There is a Bible on the table in the middle from which one of them may read. Quakers regard the Bible very highly, but they do not treat it as the final word from God. God reveals his word to individual Christians today.

A Quaker meeting house is very plain and simple. There are no ornaments or visual distractions. The seats are simply arranged facing the central table. There is no font or baptistry in a meeting house and the table is not a communion table. Friends believe that baptism is an inward spiritual experience and that there is no need for an outward ceremony or ritual. Communion is for them communication with God through the Spirit and there is no need for bread and wine.

Activities

1 Hymn-singing has always been a popular aspect of worship. Look at a number of well-known hymns. Write a hymn that might be used in Christian worship. **PS 2.1, 2.2**

2 Visit the websites of one or more of the traditions referred to in this chapter, for example: www.methodist.org.uk; www.urc.org.uk; www.baptist.org.uk; www.quakers.org.
What beliefs and principles are stressed on each of these sites? **IT 2.1, 2.2**

Key points

- Methodist, United Reformed and Baptist churches are pulpit-centred because reading and preaching the Word of God is central to their worship.

- Methodists and United Reformed members practise infant baptism.

- Baptists practise believers' baptism by total immersion.

- When Quakers meet, they wait in silence for the Spirit of God to move them with a word for the meeting.

- A Quaker meeting place is simple with a central table.

Exam tips and practice questions

Below are some sample exam questions about the Church and places of worship. Questions **1** and **2** include examiner's tips to give you hints on how to score full marks. Questions **3** and **4** are for you to try on your own.

1 Why do Catholics look upon the Pope as an important authority? *(8 marks)*

2 Is it important to Roman Catholics that a place of worship is as beautiful as possible? Give reasons for your answer, showing you have considered more than one point of view. *(5 marks)*

Try to answer the following questions on your own. Before you write your responses, think about your own hints on how to score full marks.

3 Choose one Christian tradition.

    a Describe the inside of a place of worship used in this tradition. *(6 marks)*

    b In what ways is the design of the building influenced by the worship that takes place there? *(4 marks)*

4 'A sense of vocation is an essential part of being a Roman Catholic.' Do you agree? Give reasons for your answer, showing you have considered more than one point of view. *(5 marks)*

How to score full marks

The examiner would be marking on the basis of levels of response (see page vi), so make sure your responses are full and accurate.

1 This is a question testing knowledge and understanding. You should show that you know what authority the Pope has and understand why he has that authority. You should make sure your answer allows for the way in which the Pope's authority relates to that of the Church as a whole (magisterium).

2 An evaluation question. As always, answer fully, considering as many different viewpoints as you can.

Pilgrimage and Holy Communion

This section includes:

- Pilgrimage
- Pilgrimage to the Holy Land
- Background to Holy Communion
- The importance of Holy Communion
- Celebrating the Eucharist – Roman Catholic
- Celebrating the Eucharist – Other traditions.

Pilgrimages (journeys to sacred places) are a popular and important aspect of a Christian's spiritual life. In this section you learn about why people make pilgrimages and about some of the places to which they go.

At the Last Supper, Jesus took bread and wine and gave it to his disciples. He told them that the bread and the wine were his body and blood. He said, 'Do this in memory of me.'

Almost all Christian traditions have Communion services where the bread and wine are taken in memory of Jesus. Christians understand the Eucharist in different ways and how they celebrate it reflects differences of belief. This section includes the Roman Catholic Mass and the rites of other traditions. Not all worship is Eucharistic or liturgical. The section looks at non-liturgical worship as well.

Pilgrimage

Key terms

Pilgrimage a journey to a holy place

What is a pilgrimage?

A **pilgrimage** is a journey to a holy place. The place is usually where events have happened in the past that are relevant or important to what the **pilgrim** believes.

Pilgrimage is an ancient custom but it has changed over the years. Once a pilgrimage could be a long and dangerous journey. Now travel is much easier and much less demanding. While some pilgrims still travel on foot, most travel by air or some other modern form of transport.

About 600 years ago a pilgrimage from London to the shrine of Thomas Becket in Canterbury was a major undertaking. Nowadays, pilgrims from Britain can make a pilgrimage to Lourdes in a day.

Why do people go on pilgrimages?

People go on pilgrimages for the following reasons:

- As a spiritual discipline. Pilgrimage is an act of prayer and devotion, something undertaken for God.
- As a way of increasing their faith. They visit the scenes of events that are part of their spiritual life.
- To allow those events to become more real to them. As they see the places where these things happened, they feel they can picture them more clearly. They feel closer to God during their pilgrimage.
- For the experience of being a pilgrim. For a day, or for a few days, they can concentrate on their faith in a happy, relaxed way.
- For the sense of being part of a worldwide fellowship. At the most-visited pilgrimage places they are likely to meet fellow-Christians from many other countries.
- To pray for something that is of special importance to themselves or their loved ones.

Lourdes

Many Christians visit places in different parts of the world where prayers are said for those who are sick. These may be places where they believe miracles of healing have occurred. Such a place is Lourdes, a French town at the foot of the Pyrenees.

For a period of six months in 1858, a young girl called Bernadette Soubirous had a number of visions of the Virgin Mary in a grotto near to her home in Lourdes. 'The lady,' as Bernadette called her, told Bernadette to dig nearby – if she did, she would find a stream. Bernadette did as she had been told and found a spring.

In 1862, Bernadette's visions were declared authentic by the Pope, and it was said that the underground spring revealed to Bernadette had miraculous healing qualities. Since then, Lourdes has become a major pilgrimage centre. Almost three million people visit the grotto every year to pray for themselves or for others.

Lourdes, where Bernadette saw her visions.

A number of pilgrims to Lourdes have claimed to have been cured by a miracle. The authorities at Lourdes insist that a careful investigation is made before they accept that the miracle is genuine. You can read about some of these miracles by visiting the Lourdes website (see Activity **1** opposite).

A pilgrimage to Lourdes

- Almost every pilgrim to Lourdes makes a visit to the grotto where Bernadette saw her visions. There they see a statue of the Virgin Mary in the place where she appeared to Bernadette. The statue is modelled on Bernadette's description of what she saw. Pilgrims pray at the grotto, many of them using their **rosaries**, and light candles.

- Many pilgrims visit a pool fed by the stream revealed to Bernadette. The stream itself has been channelled under the altar in the grotto. Some bathe in the stream, hoping that by doing so they may receive healing. Others drink the water – there are taps through which it is piped. Pilgrims fill flasks and bottles with the water, to take home for sick relatives and friends.

- There are stations of the cross at Lourdes. Individuals or groups of worshippers make their way from station to station as part of their pilgrimage.

- Pilgrims attend Mass at one of the churches near the grotto.

- Frequently there are processions round the grotto area.

Activities

1 Visit the following websites: www.olrl.org/stories/lourdes.html and www.ewtn.com/library/mary/zlourdes.htm. Choose one healing described and summarize the account you have chosen. Is it an example of a modern miracle? Give reasons for your answer.
   IT 2.1, 2.2, PS 2.2, 2.3

2 Look again at the points under 'Why do people go on pilgrimage?' In what ways would a pilgrimage to Lourdes meet the aims described here? **PS 2.1**

Key points

- A pilgrimage is a visit to a holy place and it is made for a spiritual reason.
- There are many notable places of pilgrimage.
- Lourdes is a place of pilgrimage especially associated with healing.
- While on pilgrimage, people make a point of taking part in certain acts of worship and prayer.

Pilgrimage to the Holy Land

The experience of a lifetime

In this unit, we are going to follow a group of pilgrims as they travel round the Holy Land, the country where Jesus lived 2000 years ago. We will not just see where they go and what happened there. We will try to understand what it feels like to see the places where Jesus is said to have been born, lived, died and rose again. At each location the pilgrims do not just listen to the guide and move on. They stop for a short Bible reading and prayer that relates to an event that happened at that place.

The group leave Britain on one Monday and come back the following Monday. They have six complete days to make their pilgrimage. It is already dark when they land at Tel Aviv Airport in Israel. They travel to Galilee for a late supper before settling down for the night.

Galilee

What a wonderful surprise they have when they look out from their bedroom windows in the morning. The beautiful calm of the Sea of Galilee, with the hills rising round it is breath-taking. They spend a couple of days in Galilee. They visit Cana where, it is stated in John's Gospel, Jesus attended a marriage at which he changed water into wine. They go to Capernaum, where Jesus often preached. They visit Nazareth, where Jesus lived with Joseph and Mary, and see the vast modern church built over the grotto of the Holy Family – said to be the place where the family home and the carpenter's workplace once stood.

Pilgrims worshipping by the Sea of Galilee.

The pilgrims travel by boat across the sea. They may well celebrate the Eucharist at one of the open-air altars near the water's edge.

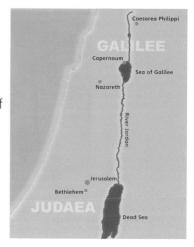

A map of the Holy Land.

From the Sea of Galilee to the Dead Sea

After a couple of days our pilgrims head south along the River Jordan. They stop at the place where it is said Jesus was baptized. A few of them have brought plastic bottles with them. They take some of the water, perhaps for the baptism of a member of the family.

The coach takes them down to the Dead Sea. It is time for recreation! Because water cannot escape from the Dead Sea, evaporation has made it very salty. Many of the pilgrims have brought their swimming costumes so that they can experience the strange buoyancy of water in which it is impossible to sink.

Bethlehem

Some pilgrims are surprised when they come to Bethlehem and find – instead of a stable – a large, richly decorated church known as the Church of the Nativity. Our pilgrims join the line of people going down a few steps into the grotto of the Nativity. There they see a silver star on the floor marking the place where Jesus is said to have been born. Pilgrims pause briefly in prayer as the line moves slowly by. They may find a place nearby for quiet prayer. The group may be able to hold an act of worship in one of the many small chapels in the church. It is a wonderful experience to worship in what is, for Christians, one of the holiest places on earth.

The traditional place of the resurrection of Jesus.

Jerusalem

The pilgrims spend two or three days in Jerusalem, where there is much to see. They visit the Western Wall, part of the site of the Temple that Jesus would have known. They also visit the places linked with the events of the days leading up to the crucifixion and resurrection of Jesus. They walk down the Mount of Olives, following the path taken by Jesus as he rode into Jerusalem on a donkey. They pass the site of Gethsemane, where Jesus prayed after the Last Supper and where he was arrested. They walk along the Via Dolorosa, the route along which Jesus carried the cross. They visit the Church of the Holy Sepulchre, in which are the traditional sites of the crucifixion and the place where Jesus was buried and rose from the dead. Pilgrims file past the sacred place, kissing the piece of marble that covers the sacred rock on which the body of Jesus lay. There is a sense of wonder as they touch the place where Jesus rose from the dead.

About 1700 years ago on a visit to the Holy Land, Queen Helena asked where certain events had taken place. The places said to be linked to the events in Jesus' life are those pointed out to her.

The Garden Tomb seems to many people to show what the burial place of Jesus would have looked like, although there is no evidence that it is the actual place.

Activities

1   Hot seat activity: invite someone who has made a pilgrimage to Lourdes, the Holy Land or another place of pilgrimage to visit the class. Ask the visitor questions, not just to find out what places are like but what it feels like to be a pilgrim. **C 2.1a, WO 2.2, 2.3**

2   Visit the websites of another place of pilgrimage such as Canterbury (www.canterbury-cathedral.org), Walsingham (www.walsingham.org.uk) or Iona (www.iona.org.uk). Why are pilgrimages made to these places? What might pilgrims do when visiting them? **IT 2.1, 2.2**

Key points

- Pilgrims to the Holy Land visit places associated with the life of Jesus and worship there.
- They walk along the routes Jesus is said to have taken on, for example, Palm Sunday and Good Friday.
- They take home memories so that in the future, when they hear about what Jesus said and did, they can picture the scenes for themselves.

Background to Holy Communion

Key terms

Last Supper the meal that Jesus shared with his disciples on the night before he was crucified

The Last Supper

Christians have always met to celebrate the last meal that Jesus shared with his disciples on the night before he died. Christians call this meal the **Last Supper**. For many, it is the main ceremony of their life as a worshipper. By sharing in a simple meal of bread and wine, Christians remember the saving power of Jesus's death and resurrection as members of the family of the Church.

The Gospel of Luke gives an account of the Last Supper.

> Jesus took bread, gave thanks and broke it, and gave it to them, saying, 'This is my body given for you; do this in remembrance of me.'
>
> In the same way, after supper he took the cup, saying, 'This cup is the new covenant in my blood, which is poured out for you.'
> (Luke 22: 19–20)

Many Christians share bread and wine together because Jesus asked his followers to do so in memory of him.

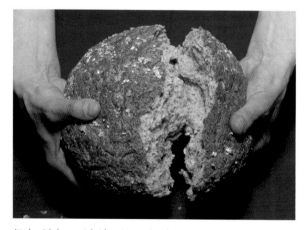

'Take it', he said, 'this is my body'.

The Jewish festival of Passover

Jesus' Last Supper with his disciples was a **Passover** meal. For Jews, Passover recalls the time early in their history when God, through Moses, saved the Jewish nation from slavery in Egypt.

The Old Testament book of Exodus describes how God sent a series of plagues on the land of Egypt to persuade Pharaoh to let the Jewish slaves go free. Nine plagues came and went, but Pharaoh refused to release the Jews. Then, following instructions from God, Moses told each Jewish household to kill a lamb and sprinkle its blood on their doorposts. During the night an **angel** came to each home in Egypt. The firstborn son in every Egyptian family died, but the angel 'passed over' the Jewish houses because of the blood on the doorposts.

Since that time, Jews have looked upon this event as the moment when their special relationship (**covenant**) with God began, sealed with the blood of the lambs.

Links between Passover and Holy Communion

Jews believe that God rescued the Jews from slavery in Egypt. Christians believe that God rescued all people from sin through Jesus Christ. His death and resurrection brought about a new covenant between God and the human race, sealed with the blood of Jesus.

Christians look upon Jesus as the Lamb of God, who sacrificed his life for the sins of the world. Sharing the bread and wine at Holy Communion is the way in which Christians remember Jesus's death and resurrection. It also enables them to celebrate being members together of the worldwide community of the Church.

Titles given to the service

The names by which the service is called vary from tradition to tradition. The names chosen reflect the various ways in which the traditions look upon the ceremony.

- **Eucharist**: this is a Greek word meaning 'thanksgiving'. By sharing the bread and wine, Christians give thanks for the death and resurrection of Jesus, and for the relationship with God that has been made possible by Jesus' sacrifice. This title is used most often by Anglicans and Roman Catholics.

- **Holy Communion**: the word 'communion' means to take part in something as a group or family. Christians meet together as a family to share the bread and wine. This title is used among Anglicans and members of the Free Churches.

- **Mass**: this title is used by Roman Catholics and some Anglicans. The service was once read in Latin and the final sentence was '*Ite, missa est*', which means 'Go, you are sent on a mission'. At the end of the service, the congregation go out to continue their Christian mission, having been strengthened by the fellowship of the Church and the body and blood of Jesus.

- **Divine Liturgy**: in this sense, the word 'liturgy' means an offering or a service. Members of the Orthodox Church use this title as they look upon the ceremony as an opportunity to offer praise to God and to give their lives to his service.

In the Free Church tradition, the sharing of bread and wine often takes place in an informal atmosphere.

- **Breaking of Bread:** some Free Church Christians prefer to use this title as it reminds them of the origin of the service. Jesus broke bread and shared it among his disciples at the Last Supper. Today, Christians share in this simple meal in memory of Jesus' death and resurrection.

- **Lord's Supper:** other Free Church Christians, such as the Baptists, prefer to use this title. In the same way as the disciples shared Jesus' Last Supper, Christians today can share in the same meal in the spiritual presence of Jesus.

Activities

1 In many cultures, sharing a meal is a sign of fellowship. Why do you think this is the case? **C 2.1a, PS 2.1, 2.2**

2 Hot seat activity: read the account of the escape of the Jews from slavery in Egypt in Exodus 12: 1–39. The teacher (or a member of the local Jewish community) answers questions from the class on the Passover meal celebrated by Jews every year. **C 2.1a, 2.2, WO 2.1, 2.2**

Key points

- Some Christians meet to remember the last meal Jesus shared with his disciples. They take bread and wine in memory of his death and resurrection.

- There are links between the Jewish festival of Passover and the Christian service of Holy Communion. In the same way as Jews believe that God rescued the Jews from slavery in Egypt, Christians believe that God saved all people from sin through the sacrifice and resurrection of Jesus.

- The Christian ceremony of sharing bread and wine is known by different titles. These titles explain the importance of the ceremony to Christians.

- Christians believe that the risen Christ is present among the community as they share a fellowship meal together.

The importance of Holy Communion

How often do Christians receive Holy Communion?

Anglican, Roman Catholic and Orthodox Christians regard Holy Communion as their principal act of worship. In most churches Holy Communion is celebrated every Sunday and often during the week as well.

Baptist, Methodist, United Reformed and other Free Churches may celebrate Holy Communion once or twice a month. Their worship is pulpit-centred and, therefore, the main emphasis of each service is on readings from the Bible and preaching.

The Salvation Army and the Society of Friends (the Quakers) do not have Eucharistic services. These Christians do not believe that outward symbols are important. They believe that the most important part of Christian worship is to accept Jesus Christ into their hearts. They honour Christ's sacrifice on the cross in the way they live their lives.

What is special about the bread and wine?

From the time of the first followers of Jesus, some Christians have believed that, at the Eucharist, they have received the body and blood of Christ. This belief is based on the words that Jesus used at the Last Supper: 'This is my body... This is my blood of the covenant which is poured out for many.' (Mark 14: 24)

Because of this, the bread and wine used at the Eucharist are special. For some Christians the bread and wine have special significance, because in some sense they become the body and blood of the risen Christ.

Such language can be puzzling, even for Christians. Throughout the history of Christianity, and in all the various Church traditions, attempts have been made to explain exactly what happens (if anything) to the bread and wine when they are blessed or consecrated. There have been

disagreements and complicated words (such as '**transubstantiation**' and '**consubstantiation**') have been used as people tried to explain it. Today there is general agreement that just how the bread and wine of the Eucharist become the body and blood of Christ is essentially a mystery. A mystery can be believed, even though it cannot be explained!

Some traditions understand the Eucharist to be a family meal. Jesus told his followers to eat and drink bread and wine in his memory and this is what they do. They believe strongly that Jesus is present among them when they meet. But they do not necessarily believe that he is present in the bread and wine or that they become his body and blood.

Some Christian traditions feel it is important to use unleavened bread (bread made without yeast), often in the form of specially made individual wafers. Jesus would have eaten unleavened bread at the Last Supper as it took place at Passover, when Jews eat this type of bread in memory of the exodus from Egypt. By eating unleavened bread and wafers, Christians are following the example of Jesus. Others are content to use ordinary bread and emphasize the significance of sharing a single loaf.

Many traditions use ordinary wine for the Eucharist, while others use non-alcoholic wine or some other fruit-based substitute. Most Churches use a single cup (**chalice**) for distributing the wine, others use small individual glasses.

The priest raises the consecrated unleavened bread, the body of Christ.

Sharing the bread and wine of the Holy Communion unites the family of the Christian Church.

Services of Holy Communion often include hymns like the one below to show the importance of the ceremony in the worshipping life of Christians.

Love is his word, love is his way,
feasting with men, fasting alone,
living and dying, rising again,
love, only love, is his way.

*Richer than gold is the love of my Lord:
better than splendour and wealth.*

Love is his way, love is his mark,
sharing his last Passover feast,
Christ at his table, host to the Twelve,
love, only love, is his mark.

Love is his mark, love is his sign,
bread for our strength, wine for our joy,
'This is my body, this is my blood,'
love, only love, is his sign.

Love is his sign, love is his news,
'Do this,' he said, 'lest you forget
all my deep sorrow, all my dear blood,'
love, only love, is his news.
(Luke Connaughton, 1917–79)

Points of agreement

Although there are differences among the traditions about the meaning of Jesus' words at the Last Supper and the frequency with which Holy Communion is celebrated, most Christians would agree on the following.

- Holy Communion is an opportunity to give thanks and praise to God for the death and resurrection of Jesus.

- At the Last Supper, Jesus asked his followers to share bread and wine in his memory and therefore **instituted** or began, Holy Communion.
- Jesus is present among Christians during Holy Communion in a real and special way.
- Christians share a fellowship meal with each other and the risen Christ.

Activities

1 Explain your answers to the following questions.
   a 'How the bread and wine of Holy Communion become the body and blood of Christ is essentially a mystery. A mystery can be believed, even though it cannot be explained.' Is it reasonable to believe in something even if you do not understand it?
   b An example of something people believe in but do not necessarily understand is electricity. Is this the same sort of mystery as the bread and wine of Holy Communion? **PS 2.1, 2.3**
2 Do you think a person can be called a Christian without taking Holy Communion? Answer this question from two different points of view. **PS 2.1, 2.3**

Key points

- Christians believe that the fellowship meal of bread and wine was instituted by Jesus at the Last Supper.
- Many Christians believe that the risen Lord is present in the bread and wine, which become his body and blood.
- In some traditions, unleavened bread is used during Holy Communion. Jesus would have eaten this at the Last Supper, a Passover meal. Other traditions use ordinary bread to emphasize the significance of sharing a single loaf.
- The Salvation Army and the Society of Friends (the Quakers) do not have services of Holy Communion.

Celebrating the Eucharist – Roman Catholic

Catholics use the terms Mass and Eucharist when speaking of Holy Communion.

Introductory Rites

- All the people make the sign of the cross and the priest greets everyone. There is a hymn and a prayer.
- The priest invites the people to reflect on what they have done wrong and to ask for God's forgiveness in these or similar words.

My brothers and sisters [or similar wording], to prepare ourselves to celebrate the sacred mysteries, let us call to mind our sins.

[After a pause, the Celebrant continues]

You were sent to heal the contrite:
Lord, have mercy.

All: Lord, have mercy.

You came to call sinners:
Christ, have mercy.

All: Christ, have mercy.

You plead for us at the right hand of the Father.
Lord, have mercy.

All: Lord, have mercy.

- The Gloria, a hymn of praise, is either said or sung by everyone. the hymn includes these words: 'Lord God, heavenly King, almighty God and Father, we worship you, we give you thanks, we praise you for your glory.'

Liturgy of the Word

There are usually three readings from the Bible.

- The first reading is from the Old Testament, the second from the New Testament (often from one of the letters of St Paul). Between the readings there is a psalm.

- Everyone stands for the reading from one of the gospels, read by the priest.
- The priest gives a homily, or sermon. It is usually based on the Bible readings.
- Everyone says the Nicene Creed.
- Then follows the Prayer of the Faithful, in which the congregation pray for the Church, the world, the local community, those who suffer or are ill and those who have died.

Liturgy of the Eucharist

- The bread and wine and the offerings of the congregation are brought to the altar in a procession. The priest offers the gifts to God. He says, 'Lord God, we ask you to receive us and be pleased with the sacrifice we offer you with humble and contrite hearts.'
- The priest washes his hands and says the Eucharistic prayer. Over the bread and wine, he says, 'Let them become for us the body and blood of Jesus Christ.'
- He takes and consecrates the bread, using the words of Jesus at the Last Supper.

The day before he suffered
he took bread in his sacred hands
and looking up to heaven,
to you, his almighty Father,
he gave you thanks and praise.
He broke the bread,
gave it to his disciples, and said:
'Take this, all of you, and eat it:
this is my body which will be given up for you.'

- He consecrates the wine using similar words, ending, 'Do this in memory of me.'
- The congregation say together the words of the Lord's Prayer.
- The priest and the congregation offer each other the sign of peace. They take the hand of the people around them in turn and say, 'Peace be with you.'

- Before receiving the bread and wine, the people ask for God's forgiveness, saying, 'Lamb of God, you take away the sins of the world, have mercy on us …'.
- The congregation receive communion. Unleavened wafers, called hosts, are used. The priest says to each communicant, 'The body of Christ' and 'The blood of Christ'. In the Roman Catholic Church, children can first receive communion from the age of seven, though the custom varies from diocese to diocese.

- Afterwards, there is a short time of silent prayer. The priest blesses the people and says,' Go in peace to love and serve the Lord.' The congregation reply, 'Thanks be to God.'

Key points

- The worshippers confess their sins as they prepare to approach God.
- The Liturgy of the Word is an important part of the Mass. It is centred on the Bible, the Word of God and on the teaching of the Church.
- The congregation pray for the world and for those in any need.
- In the Eucharist Prayer, Jesus' words at the Last Supper are used as the priest consecrates the bread and wine and they become the body and blood of Christ.

Activities

1   Watch a video of a Mass. How does it fit the pattern given here? **PS 2.1, 2.3**

2   Make up suitable intercessions to be used at the Eucharist, taking into account special needs in your area, the country and the world. **PS 2.1**

All Holy Communion services are based on the Last Supper, as is the Catholic Mass. The Anglican service is very similar to the Roman Catholic service. The main features of the rites of some other traditions are described in this unit.

Orthodox celebration

The Orthodox Church calls Holy Communion the Divine Liturgy.

Liturgy of the Word

The service begins with the **Liturgy of the Word**:

- The congregation sing hymns and pray. There is a reading from the Bible. It may be taken from the Acts of the Apostles or one of St Paul's letters.
- The priest carries the book of the gospels from behind the iconostasis towards the people. (For a description of the iconostasis, see page 33.) This is called the Lesser Entrance. The priest sings the gospel passage.
- A sermon may follow at this point. Sometimes it is given at the end of the service.

Liturgy of the Faithful

- The communion gifts of bread and wine are taken in a procession through the congregation. They are carried through the Royal Doors of the iconostasis and placed on the altar. This is known as the Greater Entrance. A member of the congregation will have baked the bread at home.
- Prayers are said for the leaders of the Church, for the world and for the local community. Everyone sings the words of the Creed and the Lord's Prayer.
- The Royal Doors are closed. At the altar, behind the doors, the priest thanks God for sending his Son to save the world. He recites the words of Jesus at the Last Supper.
- The bread is divided into four parts. One part is put whole into the chalice with the wine; the second part is divided among the clergy at the

Liturgy; the third part is cut into small pieces and placed in the chalice for the communion of the people. These three sections of bread and wine are consecrated, or blessed, by the priest to be the body and blood of Jesus. The fourth part is also cut into small pieces and placed on a dish. This section of bread is not consecrated.

- The priest invites the congregation to approach the iconostasis for communion, with words, 'In fear of God, in faith and love, draw near.' In the Greek Orthodox Church, babies and small children may receive the bread and wine as soon as they have become members of the Church through baptism and chrismation (see page 69).
- The bread and wine are given together on a spoon to each person by name. A small tray is held under the chin to catch any spillage. The mouth is wiped with a cloth. The communicant will then kiss the chalice.
- Once the congregation has received communion, prayers of thanksgiving are said. At the end of the service, the priest stands in front of the Royal Doors with the pieces of unconsecrated bread. As each member of the congregation takes a piece of the bread, they will either kiss a small cross held by the priest or the priest's hand.

The Royal Doors in the iconostasis open to allow the priest to bring the bread and wine to the people. This symbolizes breaking down the barrier of sin between God and humankind through the death of Jesus.

Baptist celebration

The Baptist communion service is more informal. It is held once or twice a month and is usually referred to as the Lord's Supper. Baptists do not use a set order of service and the pattern of the service will vary from church to church. However, the essential elements will be the same.

- The minister opens the service by inviting the people to follow the command of Jesus at the Last Supper to take bread and wine 'in memory of me'. The invitation is open to all who 'Truly and earnestly repent of their sins and are in love and fellowship with their neighbours'.

- Members of the congregation will say extempore prayers for the needs of the world and the local community. (For extempore prayer, see page 27.)

- The bread and wine are seen as symbols of his body and blood. A deacon or elder of the church says a prayer of thanksgiving for Jesus' sacrifice on the cross.

- The people remain in their seats as the deacons or elders take the bread to them. Each person takes a piece, eats it and prays in silence. Wine or grape juice is distributed in small individual cups. The congregation waits until everyone has been served and then drink together as they would at a family meal.

- The service ends with a prayer of thanksgiving. A hymn or chorus may be sung.

Methodist celebration

Methodists call the service in which they share bread and wine Holy Communion. It is held once or twice a month.

- The service opens with a hymn and prayers of praise to God.

- There is a reading from the Bible and a sermon. Prayers are said for those in need.

- The minister says the Prayer of Thanksgiving, recalling the Last Supper, over the bread and wine, 'This is my body. This is my blood.'

- The people will be invited to the communion table with the words, 'Receive the body of Christ, which was given for you and the blood of Christ, which was shed for you, and feed on him in your hearts by faith and thanksgiving.'

- The people are sent into the world to live and work to God's praise and glory.

It is usual in Free Churches for Christians to share ordinary bread in a Holy Communion service and to drink unfermented wine or fruit juice from individual glasses.

Activities

1   Why is it important to Baptists that Communion is open to all who 'are in love and fellowship with their neighbours'? Give reasons for your answer. **C 2.1a; PS 2.1, 2.3**

2   See if you can find some music used at an Orthodox Liturgy and listen to it in class. In what way would such music contribute to the atmosphere during the service? **C 2.1a; PS 2.1, 2.3**

Key points

- In all traditions that celebrate Holy Communion, the reading of scripture and prayer for anyone in need are essential parts of the service.
- Although the celebration of Holy Communion in some traditions is less frequent than in others, it is no less important.

Exam tips and practice questions

Below are some sample exam questions on Pilgrimage and Holy Communion. Questions **1**, **2** and **3** include examiner's tips to give you hints on how to score full marks. Questions **4** and **5** are for you to try on your own.

1 Choose a place of Christian pilgrimage.

  a Explain why people make pilgrimages to the place you have chosen. *(4 marks)*

  b Describe what pilgrims may do at their place of pilgrimage. *(4 marks)*

2 Describe a Roman Catholic Eucharist. Why is attending the Eucharist important to Roman Catholics? *(8 marks)*

3 Name two Christian traditions that do not celebrate the Eucharist. Why do they think it unnecessary to do so? *(5 marks)*

Try to answer the following questions on your own. Before you write your responses, think about your own hints on how to score full marks.

4 Describe what Jesus said and did when he took bread and wine at the Last Supper. *(4 marks)*

5 'Going on pilgrimage is an essential part of a Catholic's spiritual life.' Do you agree? Give reasons for your answer, showing that you have thought about more than one point of view.

How to score full marks

The examiner would be marking on the basis of levels of response (see page vi), so make sure your responses are full and accurate.

1 a A question to test your knowledge and understanding. Note that four marks are available – you must give a full explanation.

  b This question is testing your knowledge and understanding. Note that the examiner will take into account the place you have chosen. If you choose the Holy Land, you would get full marks by writing about just a few of the possible places there. If you choose, say Lourdes, there is much less to be said and it would take a fuller answer to gain full marks.

2 This question is testing both knowledge and understanding. Note the eight marks. You need to describe the whole service, not just the part surrounding the act of communion. You must also be sure to answer the second part of the question.

3 This question is a straightforward test of your knowledge and understanding.

Note that in an exam there may be a question, such as, 'Do you think people can be called proper Christians if they do not worship in church, even though they are able to do so?' You will receive no credit if you answer, 'They may be too ill to go to church or they may have to work on Sundays.' The words in the question should tell you not to write about people who are not able to go to church.

Prayer

This section includes:

- What is prayer?
- The Lord's Prayer (1)
- The Lord's Prayer (2)
- Aids to prayer (1)
- Aids to prayer (2).

This section looks at prayer, especially personal prayer. Two units are given to a study of the Lord's Prayer – the family prayer of Christians, taught by Jesus himself.

Two units are given to describing aids to prayer that are used by Roman Catholics and other Christians – among them rosaries, icons, stations of the cross and stained-glass windows

What is prayer?

Key terms

Jesus Prayer a prayer that concentrates on the name of Jesus

Meditation a quiet form of prayer in which people focus their thoughts on God

For Christians, prayer is communicating with God. That means talking to God – and sometimes listening to God.

In all relationships it is important to talk often if that relationship is to be strong and meaningful. Christians think of themselves as God's family. It is important that the family speaks to the Father.

Sometimes Christians pray in the company of others. Sometimes they pray on their own. It is an essential part of their relationship with God.

Why do Christians pray?

Christians believe in the power of prayer. They believe that God is a loving Father who wishes to help and support his children. They love God and wish to share their lives with Him. Christians believe firmly that God answers prayer.

When they pray, Christians are following the example of Jesus. In the gospels Jesus is said to have prayed often, particularly during the most challenging times in his ministry. He also taught his followers how to pray (see pages 54–6).

Christians talk to God in prayer – it is an important part of their relationship with him.

When praying, Christians feel that they are in the presence of God. They believe that they receive strength and guidance from him, which will help them in their daily lives. Prayer is an opportunity for Christians to express their love of God.

Different types of prayer

Asking God for help is an important part of prayer. But Christian prayer is more than asking for things. Jesus taught his followers that they should love God and their neighbours as themselves (Mark 12: 28–31). There are different types of Christian prayer that reflect this.

- **Adoration** – praising and honouring God ('O God, how great you are!').
- **Thanksgiving** – thanking God for everything he has given them ('Thank you, Lord, for all the good things you have given me').
- **Confession** – Christians believe it is important to repent when they have let God down in some way. Confession involves admitting what has been done wrong, saying sorry, asking to be forgiven, and promising not to do the same again ('Lord, I have sinned; forgive me').
- **Intercession** – prayer for another person or prayer about a situation that needs God's loving help and power ('Lord, please help those who have lost homes and loved ones in the earthquake').
- **Petition** – prayer for one's own needs ('Lord, I have a difficult day today. Please be with me').

Meditation

Meditation is a quiet, peaceful form of prayer. When they meditate, Christians aim to focus their thoughts on God. They may concentrate on different themes, for example, different ways of thinking about God, events in the life of Jesus and names given to Jesus. Meditation can simply be a matter of being with God. The person meditating simply sits, knowing God is there. Just as two friends or people in love are happy being together, so the person meditating is content just to be with God.

The use of the rosary is a form of meditation (see page 58). Another is the **Jesus Prayer**, which is used by many Christians, especially from the Orthodox tradition.

The Jesus Prayer

The Jesus Prayer has many forms but it is basically as written here:

Lord Jesus Christ, Son of God, have mercy on me, a sinner.

It is not a formal prayer written by somebody. It is more like a natural cry for help. It can be used for meditation, with the prayer spoken or prayed silently, perhaps in rhythm with one's breath. As people meditate on it, they think about the full depth of the meaning of each word or phrase.

The Jesus Prayer can be used as a silent 'arrow prayer' in a difficult situation. It can be used at any time, anywhere.

A Jesus Prayer from Mark's Gospel

A blind man, Bartimaeus (that is, the Son of Timaeus), was sitting by the roadside begging. When he heard that it was Jesus of Nazareth, he began to shout, 'Jesus, Son of David, have mercy on me!' (Mark 10: 46)

Ask and you will receive

Christians believe that Jesus knew God, that he was close to Him. Jesus spoke of God as a loving Father who is always at hand to listen to the prayers of his children. Jesus said:

Ask and it will be given to you; seek and you will find; knock and the door will be opened to you. For everyone who asks receives; he who seeks finds; and to him who knocks the door will be opened. (Matthew 7: 7–8)

This passage from Matthew's Gospel is not saying that God will always give people what they want. Any good parent knows not to give in to every request of their child, particularly if the request is not in the child's best interests. Christians believe that God will answer prayer in his own way, that he will do what is best in the long term for his children. They also believe that prayer is not a 'quick fix'.

A person should be prepared to work with God to achieve what is being asked for.

Activities

1 'Seven days without prayer makes one weak.' How might a Christian explain this statement? **PS 2.1**

2

'I've got an exam tomorrow, Father. Please say a little prayer for me'

Look at the illustration above. What does the teenager think prayer means? What should the priest say in reply? **PS 2.1**

3 **a** Write a prayer that includes at least two of the different types of Christian prayer (adoration, thanksgiving, confession, intercession and petition).

   b Read examples of prayers written by others in your class. Which type of prayer is being used? **PS 2.1**

Key points

- Prayer means communicating with, or talking to, God.
- There are five main types of prayer: adoration, thanksgiving, confession, intercession and petition.
- Christians believe prayer is an essential part of their relationship with God.
- Christians believe God answers prayer.

The Lord's Prayer (1)

Key terms

Lord's Prayer the prayer Jesus taught his followers to say

'Lord, teach us how to pray'

There are times when people find prayer difficult. It is not always easy to find the right words to praise God, or to ask for His guidance when things trouble us. Is it right to ask God for help with personal problems, or should our prayers be for the needs of others?

Jesus' disciples felt they needed help to pray, and they asked Jesus for his advice. They knew he was close to God and that he, himself, prayed often. Jesus answered by teaching them a prayer. As Christians call Jesus 'Lord', this prayer is known as the **Lord's Prayer**.

> Our Father who art in heaven,
> hallowed be thy name,
> thy kingdom come, thy will be done
> on earth as it is in heaven.
> Give us this day our daily bread.
> And forgive us our trespasses,
> as we forgive those who trespass against us.
> And lead us not into temptation,
> but deliver us from evil.
> For thine is the kingdom,
> the power and the glory.
> For ever and ever. Amen.

The Lord's Prayer is the most important Christian prayer – it unites the worldwide family of Christians. Members of every denomination use this prayer and it has been translated into every language in the Christian world. It appears everywhere in the life of the Church: in the Liturgy and the sacraments, in public and private prayer.

The Lord's Prayer is the ideal model for prayers of adoration, confession and petition. It enables Christians to approach God as Father whenever they feel the need to pray.

The Church of the Paternoster on the Mount of Olives, where Jesus taught his disciples the Lord's Prayer. The prayer is written on the walls in over 50 languages.

Our Father who art in heaven

In the Old Testament, when Moses approached God on Mount Sinai, he was told, 'Do not come any closer. Take off your sandals, for the place where you are standing is holy ground' (Exodus 3: 5). The people of Old Testament times looked upon God as a judge and a king, who seemed at times to be rather remote. On the other hand, Jesus called God **'Abba'**, which means 'Dad', and he encouraged his followers to do the same.

Christians believe that they can talk to God as a loving father, their heavenly father. They feel that they have a special child–father relationship with God, and can approach him in the confident way a child approaches a loving parent. In this manner, they can ask for his guidance and protection, seek his help in times of trouble, and accept his authority over their lives.

God is thought of as living in heaven. This is a way of recognizing that God is far greater than us and that he does not live on earth in the same way as we do. But Christians believe that God is near them at all times and is involved in every aspect of their lives.

Christians believe that they have a special relationship with God – they can approach him in trust, as a child would a loving parent.

Hallowed be thy name

The word 'hallowed' means 'holy'. When Christians speak of God as being holy they mean that he is far greater, more special and more powerful than anything they can imagine. He is a mystery and beyond understanding. They believe that as God is so holy, he should be honoured and worshipped.

Thy kingdom come, thy will be done on earth as it is in heaven

We normally use the word 'kingdom' to describe a place, a country ruled by a king or queen. When Christians use the term '**kingdom of God**' they are not describing a single place but anywhere God's rule is accepted over people's lives. It is a society where life is based on the love of God and of each other.

The words of the prayer suggest that in heaven God's wishes are obeyed at all times. The same cannot be said of earth, where there is often selfishness, greed, cruelty and an unwillingness to forgive. Christians believe that the kingdom cannot be built on earth through the efforts of people alone. Only God can build the kingdom, working with people who follow the example set by Jesus. Therefore, Christians pray that God will bring about a change in people's hearts, that his wishes will be obeyed on earth as they are in heaven. In this way, God's kingdom will come.

Key points

- Jesus taught his followers a prayer. It is called the Lord's Prayer.
- For Christians throughout the world it is the most important prayer.
- It is an ideal model for prayers of adoration, confession and petition.
- The Lord's Prayer is an important aspect of public and private worship.

In the first part of the Lord's Prayer, Christians praise God as Father and King. In the second part they pray for the needs of God's family, the Church. Note that the words 'us' and 'we' are used rather than 'me' and 'I'. This suggests that Christians should remember others in their prayers. They should not pray just for themselves.

Give us this day our daily bread

Bread is the basic, staple diet of many cultures. It is a word that suggests all the physical things we need to live. Although most people in the Western world rarely experience true hunger, starvation is a real possibility in other areas of the world. This phrase may be understood as asking God to ensure that all his children have enough food to survive.

There is also the need for spiritual nourishment. Christians look upon the bread of the Holy Communion as a way in which God provides spiritual strength to help them live in the way God wants.

The phrase includes the word 'this day'. Christians believe that they should ask God to provide the strength they need to face each day as it comes. There is the sense that tomorrow is another day – it is important to concentrate on today.

Forgive us our trespasses, as we forgive those who trespass against us

In this phrase the word 'trespass' is usually understood to mean 'sin' – to go against the wishes of God.

Forgiveness is an essential part of the Christian faith. Christians want to be forgiven by God when they do something they know is wrong. They believe that they must also forgive those who have offended or hurt them. There should be no room in a Christian's life for grievances or bitterness. Christians believe that they should not ask God to forgive them if they are not prepared to forgive the wrongs other people have done to them.

And lead us not into temptation, but deliver us from evil

When people are tempted they face a choice – to do what they know is right, or to do what they know is wrong. Being tempted is not necessarily wrong in itself – everyday life offers tempting choices. It is how we respond to those choices that is important.

'Give us this day our daily bread'.

Jesus faced temptation. Immediately after his baptism, he went into the desert to reflect on the work that lay ahead of him. Jesus knew that he had been sent to do God's work. He also knew that he had been given God's power to help him carry out his work. How simple it would have been to choose to use that power to make his work easier. Jesus resisted these temptations because he knew that he would be going against the will of God.

In the Lord's Prayer, Christians pray that God will give them the wisdom to make the right choices. They ask for strength to resist the temptation to go against the wishes of God.

Some Christians believe in the devil. They believe that the devil's purpose is to take people away from God by throwing temptations in their path. Other Christians look upon the idea of a devil as a symbol of humanity's natural tendency to do what they know is wrong. Whatever they think about the devil, Christians believe they need God's help when they are tempted to do wrong.

The doxology

The final section of the Lord's Prayer was added to Jesus' original prayer by the Early Church. It is called a doxology – a hymn of praise to God.

> For thine is the kingdom,
> the power and the glory.
> For ever and ever. Amen.

In the doxology, Christians thank God for the coming of his Kingdom on earth and for the strength he gives them in their daily lives. They acknowledge the existence, the power and the wonder of God in the past, the present and the future.

The Lord's Prayer ends with the word 'amen'. This means 'let it be so'. By saying 'amen', Christians are agreeing with all that has been said in the prayer. 'Amen' is a Hebrew word suggesting divine truth. In this way, by saying 'amen', Christians are also saying 'it is true' or 'it is so'.

A modern version of the Lord's Prayer
Eternal Spirit
Earth-maker, Pain-bearer, Life-giver,
source of all that is and that shall be,
Father and Mother of us all.

Loving God, in whom is heaven.
The hallowing of your name echoes through the universe!
The way of your justice be followed by the peoples of the earth!
Your heavenly will be done by all created beings!
Your commonwealth of peace and freedom sustain our
hope and come on earth.
With the bread we need for today, feed us.
In the hurts we absorb from one another, forgive us.
In times of temptation and test, spare us.
From the grip of all that is evil, free us.
For you reign in the glory of the power that is love,
now and forever. Amen.
(*Book of Common Prayer of New Zealand*)

Activities

1 Study the modern version of the Lord's Prayer. Organize a class debate for and against the following statement: 'The original words of the Lord's Prayer should not be changed. They were given by Christ himself.' **C 2.1a, PS 2.1, 2.2**

2 There are other times recorded in the gospels when Jesus prayed. Study the following verses:
   - John 11: 41.
   - Mark 14: 36.
   - Luke 23: 46.

   Why do you think Jesus prayed on these occasions? **PS 2.1**

Key points

- The Lord's Prayer encourages Christians to pray for others.
- Christians end their prayers with the word 'amen'. This means they agree with what has been said in the prayer.
- A doxology is a hymn of praise to God.

Some Christians find it helpful to focus their attention on something while they are praying. This can help them to avoid the distractions of life around them while they are talking to God. They use items such as the **rosary**, the stations of the cross and the Bible to give structure and purpose to their thoughts on God.

The rosary

The rosary is used mainly by Roman Catholics. It helps them to concentrate on their prayers.

A rosary is a set of prayer beads. As each bead is held in turn a prayer is said. There are five sets of ten beads, and each set is called a decade. The five decades are separated by larger beads. At the start of each decade the person praying says the Lord's Prayer. For each of the following ten beads the person repeats the Hail Mary (see page 15). At the end of the decade the Gloria is said.

> **The Gloria**
> Glory be to the Father
> and to the Son
> and to the Holy Spirit.
> As it was in the beginning,
> is now and ever shall be,
> world without end. Amen.

As they progress through the decades, Roman Catholics concentrate on some of the important events in the life of Jesus and of his mother, Mary. These events, called mysteries, are in groups of five.

- The joyful mysteries focus on events associated with the birth of Jesus.
- The sorrowful mysteries focus on events associated with the suffering and death of Jesus.
- The glorious mysteries focus on the resurrection and ascension of Jesus, the coming of the Holy Spirit and the receiving of Mary into heaven.

For example, the joyful mysteries are the Annunciation, Mary's visit to Elizabeth, the birth of Jesus, the presentation of the baby Jesus in the temple, and the finding of Jesus in the temple when he was twelve years old (Luke 1 and 2).

The rosary.

Icons

Icons are an important part of worship for Orthodox Christians in particular, and for some Roman Catholics and Anglicans as well. They are religious paintings of Jesus, Mary and the saints. To Orthodox Christians, they are more than an aid to prayer. They are thought to be filled with the spirit of the person represented in the picture. As such, icons are seen as being special and holy.

Every Orthodox church has icons on the walls, on stands and on the iconostasis (see page 33). The iconostasis, a screen at the front of the church, is a focal point of prayer for the congregation during the Divine Liturgy (see page 48). Orthodox Christians buy candles on entering the church. The candle is placed in front of one of the icons and the worshipper kisses the icon.

An icon.

Although Orthodox Christians treat icons with the greatest respect, they do not pray to them. The paintings help the worshipper to focus their prayers on God.

Statues

Statues are a feature of Roman Catholic and some Anglican churches. People use them to direct their attention to the person the statue represents.

- If the statue is of Jesus, they pray to him as the Son of God. The statue may direct their thoughts to a particular way of thinking of Jesus, for example, a statue of the Sacred Heart draws attention to the love of Jesus.

A statue of the Sacred Heart.

- The statue may be of Mary or another of the saints. In a church there may be a statue of the patron saint, for example, a statue of St Peter in St Peter's church. Where people direct their prayers towards the statue of a saint, they are asking the saint to pray for them and with them.

In some places it is the custom to carry a statue of a saint in procession, especially on the saint's feast day.

The lighting of candles

Candles are a symbol of Jesus, the **Light of the World**. Jesus called himself the Light of the World. The words have both the idea of a light to guide and a light that reveals secrets that people would rather hide. At many services candles on the altar or communion table are lit. Lighted candles are an important part of a number of rites. See also the units on baptism (pages 64–71), Advent and Christmas (pages 90–97) and Easter (pages 110–111).

Many Christians light candles as an aid to prayer. In Roman Catholic and some Anglican churches, Christians place a lighted candle by a statue of Jesus, Mary or one of the saints. The candles are called votive candles. They are symbols of the prayers the worshipper is offering for him or herself, or for other people. In some churches a board is placed nearby with names of those for whom prayer is requested.

Activity

Find examples of icons. What characteristics do they have in common? How are they different from other types of religious art? Can you think why they are different? **PS 2.1**

Key points

- Some Christians use certain objects to help them concentrate on prayer.
- Among those objects are rosaries, icons and statues.
- Candles are used to represent Jesus, the Light of the World.

Crosses and crucifixes

Crosses are a feature of the interior and exterior of many church buildings. On the exterior, they are statements to the community of the faith proclaimed by that Church. Inside the church they are a strong reminder of the importance of the death and resurrection of Jesus.

There are few more powerful images than the cross. Christians wear crosses and have them in their homes as a sign that they are Christians and as a focal point for prayer.

Stations of the cross

This series of pictures can be found on the walls of Roman Catholic and many Anglican churches. Each picture, or station, represents an event in Jesus' final journey to the cross. The first station recalls Jesus being sentenced to death by Pontius Pilate. The following pictures recall Jesus' suffering as he carried his cross to the place of execution. The final pictures remember his crucifixion and burial.

Although the stations of the cross can be used as an aid to prayer at any time of the year, Christians find them particularly helpful during Lent, when they prepare for the death and resurrection of Jesus at Easter. They pause at each of the fourteen stations to pray and meditate on the suffering of Jesus.

Sometimes a group of people process round the stations of the cross, with one person leading the meditation at each station.

The image of the cross is important to Christians.

A suitable meditation for the ninth station of the cross might be: 'Jesus endures weakness and agony for my sake. Help me to bear my burdens for him.'

The ninth station of the cross: Jesus falls for the third time.

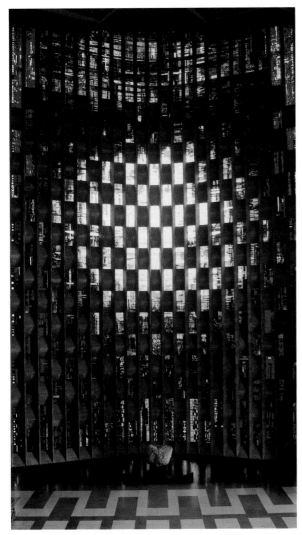

The Baptistry window in Coventry Cathedral is an abstract design that represents the light of the Holy Spirit.

Stained-glass windows

Some Christian artists, sculptors or skilled workers with glass use their talents to the glory of God. A way in which they do this in church buildings is by designing and making stained-glass windows. Traditionally, stained-glass windows were teaching aids showing stories from the Bible – remember that in the past most people could not read. Nowadays the designs may be more abstract – the aim is to create an atmosphere rather than to instruct.

The Bible

The Bible is an essential part of every Christian's life. It is not only the greatest source of information for Christians about their faith, it is also an important aid to prayer.

Many Christians of every denomination spend time each day reading a passage from the Bible. They meditate on its meaning and use it as a basis for their prayers. Christians believe that God speaks to them through the words of scripture.

Some Christians use booklets to help them study the Bible. A Bible reading is suggested for each day of the year and comments may be given to help the reader understand the deeper meaning of the passage. Other Christians may simply choose one of the books of the Bible and study it chapter by chapter on a daily basis.

Through reading the Bible and through prayer and reflection, Christians hope to learn more about God and of his will for them.

Activities

1 Are there any other items or things that could be used as aids to prayer? Give reasons for your choice. **PS 2.1, 2.2, 2.3**

2 Imagine that a side chapel in a large church is to be made into a chapel for Christian youth. Either:
   a in groups of three or four, work out the instructions to be given to the designer of the chapel's window, or
   b on your own, use the designer's instructions and produce suitable window designs.
   C 2.1a, PS 2.1, 2.2, WO 2.1, 2.2, 2.3

Key points

- Crosses and crucifixes are among the most widely used aids to prayer since they help people to focus on the crucifixion and resurrection of Jesus.
- The stations of the cross offer a further way of meditating on the death and rising of Jesus.
- Chief among aids to prayer is the Bible as a source of information and a guide to meditation.

Exam tips and practice questions

Below are some sample exam questions about prayer. Questions **1** and **2** include examiner's tips to give you hints on how to score full marks. Questions **3** to **5** are for you to try on your own.

1. Explain what Christians understand by the following phrases from the Lord's Prayer.
   a. Our Father, who art in heaven, hallowed be thy name. *(4 marks)*
   b. Forgive us our trespasses, as we forgive those who trespass against us. *(4 marks)*

2. 'To pray is to waste one's time. Nothing good comes from prayer.' Do you agree with this statement? Give reasons for your answer, showing that you have considered more than one point of view. *(5 marks)*

Try to answer the following questions on your own. Before you write your responses, think about your own hints on how to score full marks.

3

Look at the picture above. Explain carefully the meaning of what the person in the photo is doing. *(3 marks)*

4. Explain why some Christians use:
   a. a rosary, and
   b. an icon

   as aids to private prayer. *(6 marks)*

5. 'Thanksgiving is the most important type of Christian prayer.' Do you agree with this statement? Give reasons for your answer, showing you have considered more than one point of view. *(5 marks)*

How to score full marks

The examiner would be marking on the basis of levels of response (see page vi), so make sure your responses are full and accurate.

1. This is a question to test what you know. Make sure you describe clearly what each phrase means. You need to describe how these two phrases relate to a Christian's daily life. If you are not sure of the answer, pages 54–7 should help you.

2. This is an evaluation question to test how well you can assess a problem or situation. Do not write only about intercession and petition – the examiner would be looking for candidates who can write about all aspects of prayer. Make sure you include arguments for and against the statement. No more than three marks would be given for an answer that only looks at one point of view.

Christian intitiation

This section includes:

- Christian baptism
- Infant baptism
- Infant baptism services
- Believers' baptism
- Confirmation.

This section looks at baptism, which has been the Christian initiation ceremony from the time of Jesus himself. Some Christians believe that infants should be baptized and welcomed into God's family. Others believe that only those who are old enough to decide to make a true commitment to Jesus as Saviour should be baptized.

Both groups believe in baptism with water in the name of the Father, the Son and the Holy Spirit. The section includes the reasons for both infant and believers' baptism and gives an account of the rites.

Christian baptism

> ## Key terms
>
> **Baptism** to dip in or pour water over as a sign of admission into the Christian community

Baptism is an initiation ceremony – a ceremony that makes a person a member of something. In this case, someone who is baptized becomes a member of the Christian community.

A number of Christian traditions teach that baptism is a **sacrament**, an outward sign of the giving of God's grace and salvation to a person. Many Christians look upon baptism as the beginning of a life-long relationship with God.

How did Christian baptism begin?

Baptism has been an important part of Christianity since the earliest days of the Church. It has its roots in the Jewish religion. Ritual washing was a Jewish ceremony, and the Jewish Law gave instructions for bathing in running water. Jews would enter this water to make themselves ritually clean.

There are a number of occasions in the New Testament that show the importance of baptism for the early Christians.

- Mark's Gospel begins with John the Baptist. He was preaching in the desert and he had an urgent message: turn away from your sins and *be baptized*, and God will forgive your sins (1: 4).

Mark records that many people came to John in the desert to repent of their sins and to be baptized. It was a public sign that they had turned away from their old selfish lives and were making a new start.

- Jesus himself was baptized in the River Jordan.

As Jesus was coming up out of the water, he saw heaven being torn open and the Spirit descending on him like a dove. And a voice came from heaven: 'You are my Son, whom I love; with you I am well pleased.'
(Mark 1: 10–11)

Jesus was baptized at the beginning of his work for God.

Jesus' ministry was about to begin. The baptism of Jesus was an act of dedication to God and to the task ahead of him. It was a new beginning. Also, by being baptized, Jesus showed his approval of baptism.

- At the end of Matthew's Gospel, Jesus gives his final instructions to the disciples to go and make disciples of all nations, baptizing them in the name of the Father and of the Son and of the Holy Spirit. (Matthew 28:19)

From the earliest days of Christianity, baptism was seen as an important act of commitment and salvation. Those who came to believe in Jesus were to be baptized and freed from their sins.

On the Day of Pentecost, a few weeks after the ascension of Jesus into heaven, Peter spoke to a large crowd who had come to Jerusalem for the Jewish festival. He told them of Jesus, of his death and resurrection. He also appealed to them to turn away from their sins and be baptized. Many were baptized that day. (Acts 2: 14–42)

There is a clear pattern running through these stories of baptism in the early Church. One experience naturally leads to another:

- belief in Christ as the Son of God
- repentance of sins
- baptism
- God's forgiveness
- the giving of the Holy Spirit.

Baptism became an outward, visible declaration of belief, repentance and dedication to God and His son, Jesus. Unlike the cleansing rituals of the Jewish faith, Christian baptism was only to be performed once and this practice has continued to the present day. At first, those who were baptized were adults. Later, Christians wished their children to be baptized so that they too could join the family of the Church.

Baptism today

Most Christian traditions encourage baptism. It is seen as important because:

- it allows a person to make a fresh start
- sins are washed away
- people are baptized into the death of Jesus – meaning that a Christian shares in the death and resurrection of Jesus by dying to sin and rising to new life as a Christian
- it invites God into a person's life
- it gives strength to resist temptation
- it unites a Christian with other worshippers.

Many Christians believe that the gift of the Holy Spirit is given at baptism. The Holy Spirit enters the baptized person and gives new life, which is dedicated to God. The ceremony marks a new beginning in the Christian's life. It is a fresh start.

Christians believe that a person who has been baptized has been born again. Christians also say that when a person receives the Holy Spirit it brings them closer to Jesus and gives them the strength to become more like him. Through water and the Holy Spirit, baptism is a symbol of new life and salvation.

Note that Christians do not believe that the Holy Spirit can only be received through baptism. The Spirit moves freely and can come to anyone at any time.

Water is used in all Christian baptisms. Water is symbolic of two beliefs.

- As water is essential for life, so baptism brings spiritual, eternal life.
- As water is used to cleanse, so baptism brings inner cleanliness. The soul is cleansed of sin.

The Salvation Army and the Quakers do not baptize because they think it is unnecessary to have outward, visible symbols of their commitment to God. It is not the ceremony that is important, but the close relationship each believer has with God.

Water is used in all Christian baptism ceremonies – it is a symbol of new life and the washing away of sin.

Christians are baptized in one of two ways.

- pouring water on the head (see page 68)
- total immersion (see pages 70–1).

The person being baptized, or the parents and godparents, promise to turn from evil and follow Christ.

Activities

1 Are initiation ceremonies important? Give reasons for your answer. **PS 2.1**
2 Many religions use water in their rites. Why do you think this is so? **PS 2.1**

Key points

- Jesus himself was baptized.
- The apostles baptized those who joined the Church, as Jesus had told them to do.
- Baptism enables a Christian to share in Jesus' death as they do in his resurrection.
- Christians are baptized with water in the name of the Father, Son and Holy Spirit.

Infant baptism

Those who turned to Christianity in the early days of the Church wanted their children to be baptized as well. As baptism symbolizes the beginning of new life, it seemed appropriate that children should be welcomed into the family of the Church at an early age. They could then grow up surrounded by the beliefs and teachings of the Church.

Today, **infant baptism** is the most common Christian initiation ceremony. Roman Catholics baptize young children, as do Anglicans, Methodists, Orthodox and the United Reformed Church.

In most traditions, infants are baptized by pouring water on the head. In the Orthodox Church, young children are fully immersed in the water.

It is important to remember that these traditions also baptize older children and adults who were not baptized as infants. In this case, the person being baptized makes a conscious decision to be initiated into the Church. Before the baptism there is usually a period of instruction in the beliefs of Christianity and in the meaning of the ceremony. During the baptism service, water is poured on the head as it is during an infant baptism; however, the person is old enough to make his or her own promises.

The importance of infant baptism

- Many Christians believe that baptism marks the beginning of eternal life. They believe that at baptism the child is born again as a child of God. It is a new beginning.

- Baptism welcomes the child into the family of God. Many Christian parents want their children to become members of their Church's congregation from an early age. During the baptism service, they promise to provide a Christian upbringing for their child and to encourage the child to make a personal commitment to God at a confirmation ceremony when they are older (see pages 72–3).

- Baptism cleanses the child of **original sin**. It is difficult to imagine infants being capable of sin. At such a young age they do not know the difference between right and wrong. However, many Christians believe that everyone is born with the ability to sin, to go against the wishes of God. The water of baptism is seen as a sign of the Holy Spirit entering the life of the child, giving the child the strength to fight these basic instincts in later life. Christians believe that through baptism original sin is taken away.

If a child is born weak and is struggling to live, Christian parents may request that the child is baptized at the hospital. The baptism is performed on the condition that should he or she recover, the child is brought to the Church at a later date to be welcomed into the family of God.

Parents and godparents

If the person to be baptized is an infant, the statements of belief and promises to God cannot be made by the child. Parents are the most important influence on a child's life. Christian parents are responsible for making sure that the child is brought up in a Christian environment. At infant baptism, parents declare their own faith and promise to pass on that faith to their child.

To help them with this duty, godparents are chosen by the parents before the ceremony. The godparents agree to share the responsibility of educating the child in the Christian faith. Together, parents and godparents make a commitment during the ceremony to:

- provide the child with a Christian environment in which to grow up

A godparent signs the child with the cross.

- pass on the teachings of the Church
- encourage the child to attend church regularly
- teach the child about God and how to worship him
- teach the child how to pray
- set an example of Christian living
- encourage the child to be confirmed at a later date.

The following words, taken from the Anglican baptism service, describe the duties expected of parents and godparents.

> As part of the Church of Christ, we all have a duty to support *them* by prayer, example and teaching. As *their* parents and godparents, you have the prime responsibility for guiding and helping *them* in *their* early years. This is a demanding task for which you will need the help and grace of God.
>
> (The Common Worship baptism service)

Activities

1 Make a list of the criteria that should guide parents in the choice of godparents for their children. When you have finished your list, check it against the list of duties of parents and godparents. **PS 2.1**

2 To learn more about infant baptism, visit this website: encarta.msn.com Search for 'Christian baptism'. **IT 2.1**

Key points

- The majority of Christians practise infant baptism.
- Many Christians believe that through infant baptism a child is freed from original sin and made a member of the Church, the family of God.
- A commitment is made by the parents and godparents that the child will be given a Christian upbringing.

Infant baptism services

Chrismation a ceremony of anointing with oil (or chrism) immediately following baptism in the Orthodox Church

Dedication a service in which a child is brought to the Church and the parents commit themselves to bringing up the child as a Christian

Roman Catholic baptism

Baptism usually takes place during Mass.

- The child, parents and godparents are welcomed by the priest. The parents are reminded of the duties they are accepting.

> You have asked to have your child baptized.
> In doing so you are accepting the responsibility of training him/her in the practice of the faith.
> It will be your duty to bring him/her up to keep God's commandments as Christ taught us, loving God and our neighbour.
> Do you clearly understand what you are undertaking?
> **Parents: We do.**

- The sign of the cross is made on the child's forehead by the priest, parents and godparents.
- Bible readings are followed by a homily from the priest, during which the meaning of baptism is explained.
- The child is anointed with oil. This is a sign that the child is dedicated to God.

> We pray for this child:
> set him/her free from original sin,
> make him/her a temple of your glory,
> and send your Holy Spirit to dwell with him/her.
> We anoint you with the oil of salvation in the name of Christ our Saviour;
> may he strengthen you with his power, who lives and reigns for ever and ever.

- The water for baptism is blessed.
- The parents and godparents say that they reject evil and state their belief in God, Father, Son and Holy Spirit.
- Water is poured on the forehead three times. While this is being done, the priest will say, '[Child's name], I baptize you in the name of the Father, the Son and the Holy Spirit.'
- The child is again anointed with holy oil (chrism).

> As Christ was anointed Priest, prophet and King so may you live always as a member of his body.

- A white garment is put on the child.

> You have become a new creation and have clothed yourself in Christ.
> See in this white garment the outward sign of your Christian dignity.

- A candle is lit from the paschal candle and given to the child's parents. The paschal candle is a symbol of the death and resurrection of Christ.

'Bradley, I baptize you in the name of the Father, and of the Son, and of the Holy Spirit. Amen.'

Parents and godparents, this light is entrusted to you to be kept burning brightly.
This child of yours has been enlightened by Christ.
He/She is to walk always as a child of the light.
May he/she keep the flame of faith alive in his/her heart.
When the Lord comes, may he/she go out to meet him with all the saints in the heavenly kingdom.

Infant baptism in other traditions

Other traditions in which infants are baptized include the Anglican, Methodist and United Reformed Churches. In all these traditions, the child is baptized by pouring water on the forehead of the child, with the words, '[Child's name], I baptize you in the name of the Father, and of the Son, and of the Holy Spirit. Amen.'

In Orthodox baptisms, the infant is totally immersed in the water. Immediately following the baptism, there is a service of **chrismation**, in which the child is confirmed as a full member of the Church. Chrism is placed on the child's head, eyes, lips, ears, chest, hands and feet. This represents the seal of the Holy Spirit on the life of the child.

Services of dedication

Traditions that do not practise infant baptism still feel that it is important to raise children in the family of the Church. These traditions include Baptists and Pentecostal Churches. Children are brought to the Church for a service of **dedication**.

At this service, the parents and the congregation thank God for the child. The parents promise to bring up the child in a Christian environment. The congregation promise to help teach the child about Jesus Christ and Christian living. When the child grows up, he or she may choose to be baptized in a ceremony called believers' baptism (see pages 70–1).

The candle given at baptism is lit from the paschal candle to show that baptism symbolizes dying to sin and rising with Christ to new life.

Activities

1   Hot seat activity: invite a parent whose child was baptized as an infant to come to be questioned by the class. **C 2.1a , 2.1b**

2   Organize a class debate: 'How can godparents be role models to their godchildren in today's society?' **C 2.1a**

Key points

In all three traditions, there are four important elements in infant baptism:

- water
- the words of baptism: 'I baptize you in the name of the Father, and of the Son, and of the Holy Spirit
- the promises and statements of belief made by the parents and godparents on behalf of the child. In the case of an older child or adult being baptized, they will make the promises and statements themselves
- the acceptance of the child into the family of God.

Believers' baptism

Believers' baptism is practised by a number of traditions, including the Baptist and Pentecostal churches. It is the baptism of those who are old enough to make their own decision. The candidate understands the commitment being made. The method of baptism is by total immersion, usually in a pool (or **baptistry**) inside the church building, but sometimes in a river, swimming pool, sea or other running water.

The importance of believers' baptism

- Those who follow the practice of believers' baptism say that Jesus was baptized as an adult. They wish to follow his example.
- The word 'baptize' comes from the Greek term 'baptizo', meaning 'to dip'. Many Christians believe that total immersion follows the way in which the first Christians were baptized.

Evidence from the gospels

John the Baptist preached that the Messiah was coming. The message was clear:

> Turn away from your sins and be baptized, and God will forgive your sins. (Mark 1: 4)

People requested baptism as a public sign of:

- their belief
- their repentance of sin and a desire to begin a new way of life
- their wish to follow the teachings and commandments of Jesus.

The apostle Peter, in his speech on the day of Pentecost, said to all who were interested in the Christian faith:

> Repent and be baptized, every one of you, in the name of Jesus Christ for the forgiveness of your sins. And you will receive the gift of the Holy Spirit. (Acts of the Apostles 2: 38)

Today, believers' baptism follows the principle that belief in Christ comes before baptism. The ceremony is seen as important because:

- it is an outward sign of belief in Christ
- the candidate has chosen to be a Christian.

To be born again is important for those who practise believers' baptism. However, it should be noted that being born again is not part of the process of baptism for these Christians. They do not request baptism because they wish to be born again; they wish to be baptized because they have been born again.

The service of believers' baptism is an outward sign and declaration of the changes that have taken place in a person's life through belief in Jesus Christ. Following baptism, the Christian is expected to play his or her part in spreading the Christian message, avoiding sin and loving all people as children of God.

Dedication

Traditions that do not practise infant baptism still feel that it is important to raise children in the family of the Church. Children are brought to the church for a service of dedication. The parents and the congregation thank God for the child. The parents promise to bring the child up in a Christian environment. The congregation promise to help teach the child about Jesus Christ and Christian living.

Believers' baptism service

Traditions that practise believers' baptism are Churches where the worship is non-liturgical. Therefore, a service of baptism will vary a little from church to church. However, a service will contain the following points:

- The minister gives a sermon to explain the importance of baptism. It is the outward sign that a person's life has been changed by the Holy Spirit. He may call upon the congregation to remember their own baptism and to renew their commitment to Jesus Christ.

- Those who wish to be baptized are called forward. There are usually a number of candidates and each one is called forward in turn. They often wear light or white clothing. This symbolizes forgiveness and new life.

- The candidates are asked if they have repented of their sins and if they have faith in the Lord Jesus Christ.

- Each candidate may read a short passage from the Bible that is important to them. They may also give a **testimony**. This is a brief account explaining how they came to be a Christian and why they wish to be baptized.

- The candidate and minister step into the pool. The minister says, 'Name, because you have repented of your sins and have requested baptism, I now baptize you in the name of the Father, and of the Son, and of the Holy Spirit. Amen.' At this point, the candidate is briefly immersed under the water. This is a sign that the old way of life has died and that the Christian is buried in the same way as Jesus was buried in the tomb.

- The candidate leaves the pool having risen to new life with Christ. As the candidate comes out of the water, the congregation may sing a hymn or chorus chosen by the candidate. A friend, or sponsor, will be waiting with a towel. This person will have been chosen by the candidate as someone who has been important and supportive in his or her spiritual life. The candidate is led off to change and will then return to the service.

Baptism by total immersion.

Activities

1 The service of infant and believers' baptism have a number of features in common. Can you identify these common features? **PS 2.1**

2 Hot seat activity: A person who has experienced believers' baptism (who can be a member of the group) is questioned by the students. **C 2.1a, 2.2b; WO 2.1, 2.2**

Key points

- Christians who practise believers' baptism claim that they are following the example of Jesus and the early Church.

- Believers' baptism is by total immersion.

- It is the baptism of Christians who have chosen to be baptized. Candidates understand the commitment being made, and wish to dedicate their lives to Christ. Each may give a testimony, which explains how they came to be Christians and why they wish to be baptized.

- Candidates are baptized in the name of the Father, the Son, and the Holy Spirit.

Confirmation

What is confirmation?

Infants and young children cannot speak for themselves, nor is it their choice to be baptized. When they are older, they may wish to make their own promises to God and to commit themselves to following the Christian way of life.

Christians are given the opportunity to do this at a **confirmation** service. During this service, candidates are able to affirm, or agree to, the promises made on their behalf at their baptism by their parents and godparents.

Traditions that practise confirmation include Roman Catholic, Anglican, Orthodox, the United Reformed Church and some Methodist churches.

Why is confirmation important?

Confirmation is a Christian initiation ceremony. At confirmation the person being confirmed receives the Holy Spirit in a special way. During the service there is a ceremony of the laying on of hands. The president of the ceremony lays hands on the head of each candidate in turn, thus conferring the gift of the Holy Spirit. Christians believe that the Holy Spirit confirms them – he strengthens them and gives them the courage to practise their faith and teach others about Jesus.

Confirmation often takes place during a Eucharist, when the people being confirmed receive Holy Communion.

At what age is a person confirmed?

The age at which people are confirmed varies among the traditions and sometimes within the traditions themselves.

In the Orthodox Church, infants or young children are confirmed immediately after baptism.

This ceremony is known as chrismation. Oil, or chrism, is placed on the child's head, eyes, lips, ears, chest, hands and feet. These are the marks of the Holy Spirit. The bread and wine are then given to the child (see page 69).

Roman Catholics often receive Holy Communion for the first time at the age of seven, though the minimum age varies from diocese to diocese. Confirmation follows at a later date when the person is older and understands the promises and commitment being made, for example, when he or she is ten or eleven years old (or even older).

Anglican, Methodist and United Reformed Church Christians may be confirmed from the age of ten or eleven years. In these traditions admission to Holy Communion usually follows confirmation.

Preparing for confirmation

Christians who show an interest in being confirmed are invited to attend a pre-confirmation course. Candidates explore together:

- the basic beliefs of Christianity
- the meaning and importance of the Eucharist
- the value of regular Bible study and prayer
- the ways in which Christians worship God
- the standards by which Christians should live
- the promises and commitment made at confirmation.

Those who are confirmed each choose an extra Christian name, a saint's name. That name is used by the bishop when confirming them.

Roman Catholic confirmation service

A bishop normally presides at the service. However, on some occasions, the bishop may delegate his authority to confirm to a priest. He may do so especially at Easter or Pentecost, since these dates are particularly favoured days for confirmation.

- In baptism, Christians die to sin and rise again to Christ. The link between baptism and confirmation makes Easter a most suitable time.

- Pentecost is the celebration of the Holy Spirit, who came first to the Church at Pentecost and comes to the individual Christian at confirmation.

The ceremony usually takes place during the Eucharist.

- After prayers and Bible readings concerning the Holy Spirit, candidates for confirmation are called by name and asked to stand. The bishop speaks to them about the importance of confirmation.
- They repeat the promises made by themselves or by parents and godparents at their baptism.
- The bishop extends his hands over those who wish to be confirmed and prays that they may be given the gifts of the Holy Spirit.

> Send your Holy Spirit upon them
>   to be their Helper and Guide.
> Give them the spirit of wisdom and
>   understanding,
>   the spirit of right judgement and
>   courage,
>   the spirit of knowledge and reverence.
> Fill them with the spirit of wonder and awe
>   in your presence.

- Each candidate approaches the bishop in turn, together with their sponsor. The sponsor places a hand on the candidate's shoulder as a sign of support. Placing his hand on the candidate's head, the bishop makes the sign of the cross with oil, or chrism, on the candidate's forehead.

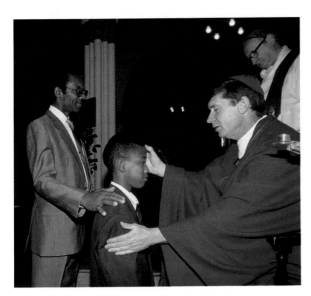

Anointing with chrism.

The anointing is the central action of the ceremony.

- The bishop says, 'Be sealed with the Gift of the Holy Spirit.' He may gently tap the candidate's cheek in welcome. The candidate makes a fresh start in the Christian life.
- After each candidate has been confirmed, the service of the Eucharist continues.

Activities

1   'A girl of sixteen has just been confirmed. She asks herself the question. "I want to be a better Christian at school. How am I going to achieve this?"'

    Divide the class into groups. Each group should think of three targets the girl could set herself. The groups should then report back to the class, explaining why they have chosen their particular targets.
    C 2.1a, 2.1b; WO 2.1, 2.2, 2.3

2   'Public ceremonies of commitment are important if Christians are serious about their faith and beliefs.' Do you agree with this statement? Give reasons for your answer. **PS 2.1, 2.3**

Key points

- At confirmation, Christians make for themselves the promises made on their behalf at their baptism by parents and godparents. They commit themselves to following the Christian way of life as adult members of the Church.
- Christians believe that they receive the Holy Spirit in a special way at confirmation. The Holy Spirit gives them the courage and strength to practise their faith.
- There is usually a period of instruction before confirmation.
- Candidates are confirmed by the laying on of hands. In some traditions this is performed by a bishop.

Exam tips and practice questions

Below are some sample exam questions about Christian initiation. Questions **1** and **2** include examiner's tips to give you hints on how to score full marks. Questions **3** and **4** are for you to try on your own.

1

Look at the picture above.

a Explain what is happening. *(2 marks)*

b What commitment will the person being baptized have made? *(4 marks)*

c Suggest two reasons why some Christians believe people should be baptized in this way. *(4 marks)*

2 Describe an infant baptism in a Roman Catholic Church. Pay particular attention to the words of the rite. *(8 marks)*

Try to answer the following questions on your own. Before you write your responses, think about your own hints on how to score full marks.

3 What is the importance of confirmation for Roman Catholics? How is that importance shown in the way in which candidates prepare for confirmation and in the rite itself? *(6 marks)*

4 Do you think a Quaker could accept an invitation to be a child's godparent? Give reasons for your answer, showing you have considered more than one point of view. *(5 marks)*

How to score full marks

1 This is a question to test what you know. It would be marked on a point-by-point basis (see page vi). In both **b** and **c** there are some detailed points that will, if clearly made, receive two marks rather than one.

2 This answer will need continuous writing and will be marked by levels by response. Note that the examiner expects you to write about the words, as well as the actions. You are not expected to learn the words by heart (though you should know the actual words used as the person is being baptized). You should have an idea, for instance, what is said to the parents and godparents about their duties.

Other rites of passage

This section includes:

- Marriage
- The marriage ceremony
- Marriage vows
- Life after death
- Funerals.

The section covers the meaning of Christian marriage. It describes the Roman Catholic ceremony and other marriage ceremonies, putting particular emphasis on the vows made by the bridegroom and bride.

It also covers Christian beliefs about life after death and shows how the Requiem Mass and other funeral rites reflect those beliefs.

Marriage

To Christians, **marriage** is part of God's plan for the human race. They may not believe that the creation happened as described in the first chapter of the Bible. They do believe that these verses contain an important truth.

> So God created human beings in his own image, in the image of God he created them; male and female he created them. God blessed them and said to them, 'Be fruitful and increase in number.' (Genesis 1: 27–8)

So Christians believe that because of the way God created human beings:

- it is natural that a man and a woman should be attracted to each other and come to love each other
- because of their love for each other they marry and thus become a family
- the husband and wife have sexual intercourse and children are born. It is one of God's greatest gifts to the human race that, in almost every case, when children are born they are surrounded by people who love them.

Jesus's teaching about marriage

When Jesus was asked about the Old Testament law relating to divorce, he quoted from Genesis.

> At the beginning of creation God 'made them male and female'.
> For this reason a man will leave his father and mother and be united to his wife, and the two will become one flesh. So they are no longer two, but one. Therefore what God has joined together, let man not separate. (Mark 10: 6–9)

Christians find it significant that Jesus performed his first miracle when he changed water into wine at a wedding (John 2: 1–11). They believe that when Jesus performed miracles, it was not just to impress people but to meet real human need. Health is important – Jesus healed those who were ill or disabled. It is important that people have food – Jesus fed hungry people. The death of a loved one is a terrible blow – Jesus restored dead people to life. Jesus turned water into wine because marriage is important – it mattered that the couple married at Cana had a good start to their married life, not one that would have everyone laughing at them. The fact that Jesus performed this miracle is a sign that marriage is important in the eyes of God.

Love

Christians teach that the starting-point of every marriage should be love. The couple should feel so attracted to each other that they believe their marriage will last for life.

Jesus taught that people should love God and love their neighbours. He was speaking of a generous, caring, understanding love to be shown to everyone, even people one has never met. Love in marriage is of a different kind, given uniquely to one person. When a man and a woman give that sort of love freely to one another, there is the basis of a Christian marriage.

- The couple find each other personally attractive. They enjoy being together, talking together. They may have similar interests and like the same sort of music and other entertainment, or they may not – that does not necessarily matter.
- The couple find each other physically attractive. Sex is an expression of love and is an important part of marriage.
- The couple respect and value each other. They may or may not share the same religious beliefs or political views, or they may agree or disagree about important moral issues – the mutual respect is still there.
- The couple feel a natural fondness, a deep affection for each other. This attraction goes beyond things people can analyze. It cannot be put into words. It is simply *felt*.

Shared interests are a feature of many strong marriages.

- The couple are totally committed to each other. They know that the future may bring troubles, problems, even tragedies. They want to be together. Each person is determined to support and stand by the other, whatever life may bring.

When two people have this sort of feeling for each other, they feel they want to make a real commitment to each other. They look forward to a future together, which they hope will be long and happy.

Christian marriage

Christians see Christian marriage as an ideal. A Christian marriage is a complete commitment between two people. It is what every Christian bridegroom and bride should hope for on their wedding day.

Christians do not expect married life to be endlessly happy, free from all troubles and worries. It does not always work out as the new bride and groom wish. Some marriages do end in divorce. However, the great majority of couples on their wedding day are determined that theirs will be an ideal marriage.

Activities

1 Is it possible to be sure you love another person so much that you know this is the person for you to marry? Give reasons for your answer. **PS 2.1**

2 Think of married couples whom you know. Do they share the same interests? Do they have the same beliefs and opinions? Does it seem to matter? Give reasons for your answer. **PS 2.1**

Key points

- Christians believe that God created human beings male and female so that they would fall in love and marry.
- Jesus taught that husband and wife are joined together by God.
- The foundation of Christian marriage is love.

The marriage ceremony

Brides and bridegrooms often put a great deal of thought into planning their wedding day. Thousands of pounds are spent on things like dresses and flowers. One couple will want their wedding to be strikingly different and original, another will want everything to be traditional.

Christian couples enjoy planning their weddings just like any others. An important part of their planning is preparing for the marriage ceremony in the church. They meet the priest who is to conduct the marriage service and together they talk through the details of the service and, more importantly, the meaning of what they will say and do.

The Roman Catholic marriage service

When two Roman Catholics marry, the marriage normally takes place during a Nuptial Mass. A marriage between a Catholic and a Christian of another tradition may also take place within a Nuptial Mass if the other Christian is a regular worshipper.

The main features of the marriage service are as follows:

- The bridegroom and his best man arrive early, as do the guests. The bride and her attendants arrive last. She enters the church escorted by her father or another close relative.
- The theme of the service is love. The collect of the Mass picks up the theme.

  Father, you have made the bond of marriage a holy mystery,
  a symbol of Christ's love for his Church.
  Hear our prayers for [Name] and [Name].
  With faith in you and in each other they pledge their love today.
  May their lives always bear witness to the reality of that love.

- During the Liturgy of the Word, the readings and the homily relate to the meaning of Christian marriage.

- As the marriage rite begins, the priest reminds the couple that marriage is a sacrament, a gift of grace to help them keep their marriage vows faithfully.
- The bridegroom and bride each state that they wish to marry the other and there is no legal objection to their marriage.
- The couple are asked, 'Are you ready to accept children lovingly from God, and bring them up according to the law of Christ and his Church?' The Roman Catholic Church teaches that if a couple firmly intend and deliberately ensure that their marriage will be permanently childless (assuming the bride is young enough to bear children) then the marriage is not valid.
- They exchange rings, symbols of their unending love.

  [Name], take this ring as a sign of my love and fidelity.
  In the name of the Father, and of the Son, and of the Holy Spirit.

- Prayers are offered for the couple in their married life.
- After receiving God's blessing, they leave the church to be greeted and congratulated by family and friends.

What the rite says about the meaning of marriage

The prayers in the service say a great deal about the meaning of Christian marriage.

- Love in marriage is a reflection of the love of God.

  In the love of man and wife, God shows us a wonderful reflection of his own eternal love. Today [Name] and [Name] have dedicated themselves to one another in unending love. They will share with one another all that life brings.

Traditionally a bride is given away by her father, or some other family member or friend.

- Jesus is present with the couple through the sacrament of marriage.

  Christ is present to [Name] and [Name] in this Sacrament of Matrimony.
  We pray that he will continue to make his presence felt throughout their lives.

- Marriage is seen realistically, with its times of difficulty and stress. The couple approach the joys and troubles of marriage in the strength given by God's grace.

  May the grace given to [Name] and [Name] in this Sacrament of Matrimony
  be always active in them.
  May it inspire them when life seems dull and strengthen them in times of trial.
  May it give them understanding in moments of tension,
  and fill them with gratitude when all goes well.

- Marriage is the basis of family life. The Christian ideal is a loving family based on a secure marriage.

  May the love of [Name] and [Name] grow large enough
  to embrace the children God may send them.
  May they, in their turn, bring ever greater happiness to their parents.

- A marriage affects the lives not only of the husband and wife but also of their families.

  By this marriage our two families have been united.
  May all of us, and particularly the parents of [Name] and [Name]
  increase in affection for one another,
  and find in one another a source of help and strength.

Activities

1 Some couples choose to go away together and get married without any family or friends being present. Others say that to do this is to forget that marriage is about family and shared friendships. What are your views on this? **PS 2.1**

2 An important part of preparation for a marriage service is the choice of hymns. Look at the sort of hymn used at marriage services. Do you think they are appropriate for a marriage? **PS 2.1**

Key points

- The foundation of a Christian marriage is love.
- The husband and wife each promise to put the other partner first in their lives.
- An important part of the Christian marriage bond is sexual intercourse, reserved for the husband and wife alone.
- The couple promise to provide a secure, loving, Christian home for their children.

Marriage vows

Key terms

Vows solemn promises that should never be broken

> I call upon these persons here to witness
> that I, [Name], do take thee, [Name],
> to be my lawful wedded wife
> to have and to hold from this day forward,
> for better, for worse, for richer, for poorer,
> in sickness and in health,
> to love and to cherish,
> till death do us part.

These **vows** from the Roman Catholic marriage rite are much the same as those of other Christian traditions. The bridegroom takes the bride by the hand and makes these vows to her. He releases her hand, she takes his hand and makes her vows to him.

A tremendous commitment

The priest will have talked to the couple before the marriage ceremony about the meaning of the vows they will be making. Each should have thought about the commitment to be made to the other.

- 'For better, for worse.' Each promises the other that, even if someone who seems more attractive or desirable appears, they will still remain faithful.
- 'For richer, for poorer.' Again, each promises that they will not desert the other if someone richer turns up – or, for that matter, someone with no money who appears to be more exciting or romantic.

The two points above are also understood by some people to mean, 'in good times and bad, in prosperity and poverty'. In a sense, it does not matter, since the commitment of marriage includes all of these things.

- 'In sickness and in health.' This is a big commitment. Remember that these vows are lifelong. Should illness or accident leave one partner helpless, at any stage in life, the other is committed to caring for him or her. Even if one partner cannot cope with the physical task of nursing and, therefore, the other is taken into a nursing home, the commitment to offer care and love remains.
- 'To love and to cherish.' It may seem strange to promise to love someone. Yet in Christian marriage, that promise must be made.

People who feel unsure about whether their love will last should think very deeply about whether they should be getting married. 'To cherish' means 'to go out of your way to let your husband or wife feel really special'. A married couple should not take each other for granted. Special treats and surprises (not just at birthdays and anniversaries) are an important part of every marriage.

- 'Till death do us part.' These vows look well beyond the wedding day. The commitment to each other is to be lifelong.

These promises add up to a huge commitment to each other. The couple know that the promises are at the heart of a Christian marriage. They come to make them willingly because of their love for each other.

The rings

The bridegroom and bride exchange rings. A ring has no beginning or end. The wedding ring is a sign of unending love and faithfulness.

> [Name], take this ring
> as a sign of my love and fidelity.
> In the name of the Father, and of the Son,
> and of the Holy Spirit.

Fidelity (faithfulness) is an important part of Christian marriage. At their marriage the couple put tremendous trust in each other. Adultery is a breaking of that trust and can have a devastating effect on the person who feels betrayed. The bride and bridegroom promise to be faithful throughout their lives.

Wedding rings are symbols of unending love.

To love, cherish and obey

In older forms of the marriage service, the bride promised to obey her husband. Nowadays it is optional whether she says she will obey.

The meaning is not that the wife should be her husband's slave! In any case, if the husband loves his wife, he will not ask anything unreasonable of her. Those brides who do choose to say 'obey' do so as an act of trust in the love that they share.

In practice, husbands and wives do not give orders to each other. They ask each other to do things – and, because of their love for each other, they will try to do what the other asks.

Activities

At a register office marriage, the bridegroom and bride each make two statements.

- I do solemnly declare that I know not of any lawful impediment why I, [Name], may not be joined in matrimony to [Name].
- I call upon these persons here present to witness that I, [Name], do take thee, [Name], to be my lawful wedded wife/husband.

1 How do these statements differ from the Christian marriage vows? **PS 2.1, 2.2**

2 Which vows do you think are more suitable for a modern marriage – the Christian marriage vows or those made at a register office? Give reasons for your answer. **PS 2.1, 2.2**

Key points

- Christian marriage vows contain a total commitment to each other by the bridegroom and bride.
- The rings are signs of lifelong love and faithfulness.

Life after death

What Jesus taught

Jesus taught that there is life after death. The reason why he, the Son of God, became human, suffered, died and rose again was to make it possible for those who had faith in him to share in the joys of heaven after they had died.

> God so loved the world that he gave his one and only Son, that whoever believes in him shall not perish but have eternal life.
> (John 3: 16)

Jesus taught about the effect of his death and resurrection in many ways. He often spoke of the way in which life springs from a seed. For example, a few days before the crucifixion and referring to the effect of his own death, he said:

> I tell you the truth, unless a grain of wheat falls to the ground and dies, it remains only a single seed. But if it dies, it produces many seeds.
> (John 12: 24)

When Jesus was on the cross, one of the thieves said to him 'Jesus, remember me when you come into your kingdom.' Jesus answered him, 'I tell you the truth, today you will be with me in paradise' (Luke 23: 42–3). He was telling the thief that there is a life after death and that they would be together in heaven when, in an hour or two, they died.

New life springs from a seed.

The message of the first Christians

Jesus' followers made it a key point in their teaching that, because of his death and resurrection, those who accept him as Saviour will receive eternal life in heaven. Without that hope the Christian faith is nothing. As Paul wrote (1 Corinthians 15: 12–19), if there is no resurrection then Christians are wasting their time. Because Jesus did rise, Christians believe they have a guarantee that there is a life to come.

A vision of heaven

Revelation, the last book of the Bible, is a vision of heaven, as described by John the Divine (who may or may not be the same John who wrote the fourth gospel). In places it is a difficult book to understand and explain. There is a clear description of those who are citizens of the New Jerusalem in heaven.

> They will be his people, and God himself will be with them and be their God. He will wipe every tear from their eyes. There will be no more death or mourning or crying or pain, for the old order of things has passed away.
> (Revelation 21: 3–4)

What comes through most strongly is that after death those who have followed Jesus will be with God. Being with him is the all-important part of being in heaven.

Purgatory

Some Christians, including Roman Catholics, believe in purgatory. Purgatory is understood to be a state of waiting for heaven, a time of cleansing from sin and preparing to enter heaven. People pray for those who have died, asking that God will have mercy on them and that their sins may be forgiven. The Roman Catholic funeral rites (see page 84) are firmly focused beyond the time of waiting and concentrate on the hope of heaven.

Belief in eternal life

A belief in life after death is important to Christians. It is this belief that makes the Christian faith relevant to people today.

- It helps them to make sense of the fact that in many ways life seems unfair. People sometimes ask why life is easy for some people while others have to face great suffering. Much human suffering is caused by other human beings. Jesus did not promise that there would be no suffering for his followers. He himself suffered unjustly through the actions of other people. Jesus promised his followers peace and happiness in the life that follows death.

- It gives them support when they are bereaved. Christians believe that, because death is not the end, they can entrust their loved ones to the love and mercy of God.

- It gives them an extra purpose in living. Christians believe that one day they will be judged, like everyone else. Even though they have done wrong in their lives, they believe that, because Jesus died to save them, their sins can be forgiven. Jesus has promised that those who love and serve him will be welcomed into the kingdom of God.

A Christian facing death

David Watson, a popular preacher who knew he was dying of cancer, wrote:

> The Christian is not preparing for death. Essentially he is preparing for life, abundant life in all its fullness... When I die, it is my firm conviction that I shall be more alive than ever... The actual moment of death is shrouded in mystery, but as I keep my eyes on Jesus I am not afraid. Jesus has already been through death for us, and will be with us when we walk through it ourselves.
>
> (*Fear No Evil* by David Watson)

'In loving memory of John William Matts, who died April 29th 1974, aged 72 years. Till we meet again. Also his wife Mary, who died October 27th 1983, aged 81 years. May she rest in peace'

Activities

1 Look at obituary notices in a newspaper or inscriptions on tombstones in a graveyard. Do the words show any belief in life after death? If so, what beliefs are there? Would you say they are Christian beliefs? **PS 2.1**

2 Read the following last words, spoken by three different people.
- Die, my dear doctor? It is the last thing I shall do! (*Lord Palmerston*)
- Why fear death? It is the most beautiful adventure in life. (*Charles Frohman*)
- See in what peace a Christian can die. (*Joseph Addison*)

What attitudes to death and life after death do these statements show? **PS 2.1**

Key points

- Jesus taught that there is life after death.
- Because Jesus died to take away sin, that life will be with God for those who accept Jesus as their Saviour.
- Belief in a life with God after death, both for oneself and for one's loved ones, makes the Christian faith relevant to people today.

Funerals

What a Christian funeral means

A Christian **funeral** looks both backwards and forwards.

- The main theme of a funeral is trust in God. Christians believe that there is hope of a future life because Jesus died on the cross to take away the sins of the world. Through his death his followers can hope that their sins will be forgiven and that they may be with God in heaven.
- The funeral looks to the future life in heaven. The mourners pray for the person who has died, entrusting their loved one to the love of God.
- The service is also a celebration of a life. Many families approach the funeral of a loved one in a very positive way. The mourners look back over the dead person's life. They remember the lovable characteristics of the deceased and the good times they enjoyed.
- It is a time of sadness and loss. Everyone attending a funeral understands the feelings of the close family. Not only have they lost someone they love deeply; for some it may mean a huge change in their everyday lives. The future may seem uncertain. The time after the funeral can be lonely and stressful – while for everyone else life goes on as before, their lives will never be the same again.

A Roman Catholic funeral

- A Roman Catholic funeral usually takes place as part of a Eucharist. The service is known as a Requiem Mass. *Requiem* is a Latin word meaning 'rest' from the opening words of the Latin Mass used at a funeral – 'Rest eternal grant unto them, O Lord'.
- The coffin may be brought to rest in the church overnight before the funeral.

- The priest meets the cortège (the procession of the coffin followed by the chief mourners) at the church door. The coffin is often sprinkled with holy water. The priest leads the cortège into the church. The Entry Antiphon is said or sung.

  Eternal rest grant to them, O Lord
  and let perpetual light shine upon them.

- Mass is celebrated with the readings and prayers focused on the Christian hope of eternal life.
- The homily normally includes a tribute to the person who has died. The preacher also speaks of everlasting life for those who trust in the death and resurrection of Jesus.
- The Eucharistic Prayer speaks of the Christian hope and asks that the person who has died may be among those who enter heaven.

  In him, who rose from the dead,
  our hope of resurrection dawned.
  The sadness of death gives way to the bright promise of immortality.
  Lord, for your faithful people life is changed, not ended. When the body of our earthly dwelling lies in death we gain an everlasting dwelling place in heaven.

  Remember [Name]
  In baptism he/she died with Christ:
  may he/she also share his resurrection,
  when Christ will raise our mortal bodies
  and make them like his own glory.
  Welcome into your kingdom our departed brothers and sisters, and all who have left this world in your friendship.
  There we hope to share in your glory
  when every tear will be wiped away.

- The funeral is followed by burial or **cremation**.

Funerals in other traditions

A funeral service may take place in the family's usual place of worship or in a cemetery chapel or **crematorium**. The pattern is very much the same.

A crematorium chapel.

- The coffin is brought into the church or chapel. The minister leads in the coffin and the mourners.
- The service includes readings from the Bible about eternal life and usually a tribute or eulogy, a speech in which either the minister or someone who knew the dead person well speaks about the life that has ended. If the eulogy has been delivered by a friend or relative, the minister may, in a sermon, speak of the Christian hope.
- Prayers are said to give thanks for a person's life and to ask God to forgive their sins and to receive their soul. They also pray for comfort and support for those who mourn the death of loved ones.
- The committal, the point when the body is committed for burial or cremation, comes at the end of the service.

Burial or cremation?

It does not matter to Christians whether a person is buried or cremated. Either way, the person's body is treated with respect.

- If the body is to be cremated then, if the service is in a crematorium, the body is committed for cremation there and then.
- If the service has taken place somewhere else, the coffin is taken to the crematorium. The committal takes only a few minutes.
- If the body is to be buried it is taken to the churchyard or cemetery. It is lowered into the grave. The prayers for the committal are said.

Relatives and friends throw handfuls of earth into the grave, symbolizing that they are sharing in the act of laying their loved one to rest.

All-merciful Father, we commend the soul of this our brother/sister into your hands. We are strengthened by the sure hope that he/she, together with all who have died in Christ will rise again with Christ on the last day. We thank you for all the blessings with which you endowed this servant of yours in his/her life on earth. They are for us too a token of your love, and of the blessed union of the saints in Christ. Listen, then, Lord, in your mercy to our prayers that the gates of paradise may be opened to your servant and that we who are left may console one another with words of faith until we all meet in Christ and are with you and our brother/sister eternally. Through Christ our Lord. Amen.

(Prayer used at the committal in a Roman Catholic Funeral Mass)

Activities

1 Read the prayer used at the committal in a Roman Catholic Funeral Mass. In what ways does the prayer sum up the themes of the service? **PS 2.1**

2 Look at one or two hymns that are often sung at funerals (for example, *Abide with me*, *The Lord's my Shepherd*). You will find these in a hymnbook. Why do people choose hymns like these? **PS 2.1**

Key points

- A Christian funeral focuses on the hope of eternal life based on faith in the power of the death of Jesus.
- Prayers and readings stress the hope of eternal life.
- The service includes thanksgiving for the life just ended and prayers for those who mourn.

Exam tips and practice questions

Below are some sample exam questions about rites of passage. Questions **1** and **2** include examiner's tips to give you hints on how to score full marks. Questions **3** and **4** are for you to try on your own.

1 Describe a Roman Catholic marriage service, paying particular attention to what is said. *(8 marks)*

2 Look at the illustration of a headstone on page 83. Do you think the stone shows a Christian belief in life after death? Give reasons for your answer, showing you have considered more than one point of view. *(5 marks)*

Try to answer the following questions on your own.

3 Read the following hymn.

Lord of love and life,
blessing man and wife:
as they stand, their need confessing
may your hand take theirs in blessing;

you will share their life –
bless this man and wife.

Lord of hope and faith,
faithful unto death:
let the ring serve as a token
of a love sincere, unbroken,
love more strong than death –
Lord of hope and faith.
(Basil E Bridge, *Hymns for Today's Church*, Jubilate Hymns)

In what ways do these verses illustrate the principles of Christian marriage? What aspects of Christian marriage are not contained in them? *(6 marks)*

4 'Despite the fact that 40 per cent of marriages end in divorce, the ideal of Christian marriage is as important as ever.' Do you agree with this statement? Give reasons for your answer, showing you have considered more than one point of view. *(5 marks)*

How to score full marks

1 This is a question to test what you know. It would be marked on a point-by-point basis (see page vi). For full marks, virtually every significant point would need to be covered, especially with regard to the vows and what the service says about the meaning of Christian marriage. Check the vows on page 80 carefully to make sure your answer is complete.

2 This is an evaluation question to make you think and to test your judgement. The examiner would be marking on the basis of levels of response (see page vi). Make sure you look at every part of the design.

You need not comment on the names, dates and ages – you should think about the words and the other parts of the design. Do the flowers mean anything? Is anything missing (for example, is there any sign of Jesus as Saviour)?

Note that Christians do *not* believe in reincarnation. Reincarnation means that a person returns to earth and lives again as somebody or something else. This is not a Christian belief and you will lose marks if you say that Christians do believe in reincarnation.

The Christmas cycle of festivals

This section includes:

- Advent
- Christmas
- Advent and Christmas customs
- Epiphany.

This section looks at the festivals and the special days and seasons that relate to the celebration of Christmas. It covers the season of Advent and the celebration of Christmas, together with ceremonies and customs that relate to one or both. It moves on to the celebration and the message of Epiphany.

Advent

What is Advent?

The season of **Advent** begins on the fourth Sunday before **Christmas** and ends on Christmas Eve. The word 'Advent' means 'coming'. It is a time of preparation for the birth of Jesus Christ. For Christians, Advent is filled with the spirit of expectation and anticipation. It is also a time of thoughtful preparation and prayer as Christians ready themselves spiritually for the festival of Christmas.

The second coming

During Advent, Christians think about the coming of Jesus as an infant in Bethlehem. They also think about the second coming of Christ (the **Parousia**). Jesus promised his followers that he would return to the world one day in glory as God the Son and as judge and king. He will return in such glory that no one will doubt that he is God the Son. The Parable of the Sheep and the Goats describes Christ's second coming. (Matthew 25: 31–46).

A time of watching and preparation

The expectation of Advent is expressed well in the Parable of the Ten Bridesmaids, who are anxiously awaiting the arrival of the bridegroom. There is deep joy and anticipation at his expected coming. There is also a warning of the need for preparation for his arrival (Matthew 25: 1–13).

In the same manner, Advent for Christians is a time of joyful expectation and careful preparation for Christmas. This is shown in such customs as the Advent wreath or ring, Advent candle and Advent calendar. These customs are followed in church and at home.

The Advent wreath

The Advent wreath, sometimes called the Advent ring, is a popular symbol in many churches and homes throughout the season of Advent. It is a circle of evergreen leaves with five candles – one in the centre and four around the outside. The centre candle, sometimes called the 'Christ Candle', is white. This is the colour of joy. The other candles are usually purple or blue, the colours of penitence.

The wreath's circle reminds Christians of God's endless love and mercy. The evergreen leaves represent the hope of eternal life brought by Jesus Christ. The candles symbolize the light of God coming into the world through the birth of Jesus Christ.

On the first Sunday in Advent, and during the week that follows, one candle is lit. On the second Sunday two candles are lit. This continues throughout the four Sundays in Advent. As the candles are lit, a passage from the Bible may be read and a prayer said. As the weeks pass, the wreath becomes brighter – the birth of the Light of the World is near. The white candle in the centre is lit with the other candles on Christmas Day and in all services during the twelve days of Christmas (see pages 92–3).

Many churches use the Advent wreath as a teaching aid during the season. It helps to focus the minds of the congregation on their spiritual preparation for Christmas. Often, members of the congregation are invited to light the candles and read an appropriate Bible passage.

Lighting the Advent wreath.

An Advent candle.

A traditional Advent calendar.

Advent candle

An Advent candle can be found in many Christian homes during this period. The candle has the numbers 1 to 24 equally spaced along its length. Every day during Advent, the candle is lit and burnt down to the next number. In many homes, a reading from the Bible and a prayer accompanies the lighting of the candle.

Advent calendar

An Advent calendar counts the days to Christmas. It is usually made of card with a seasonal picture on the front. There are 24 numbered windows and one window is opened each day during Advent. Traditional Advent calendars have a picture or short Bible text associated with Christmas behind each window. They help children to concentrate on the Christian message of Christmas.

Advent prayers

The prayers used in many churches during Advent reflect the themes of preparation and watchfulness.

> Lord our God, keep us your servants alert and watchful as we await the return of Christ your Son, so that, when he comes and knocks at the door, he may find us vigilant in prayer, with songs of praise on our lips.
> (*Methodist Worship Book*)

Activities

1. Read the Advent prayer. Identify the phrases in the prayer that reflect the different themes of the season of Advent. **PS 2.1**
2. Some people think that the true meaning of Advent has been spoilt by the emphasis on Christmas shopping, Christmas food, and the commercialization of the festival. Organize a class debate on this. **C 2.1a, 2.1b**
3. Read the parable of the Sheep and the Goats (Matthew 25: 31–46). How does this passage describe the second coming of Christ? **PS 2.1**

Key points

- The word 'Advent' means 'coming'.
- The season of Advent begins on the fourth Sunday before Christmas. For Christians, it is a time to prepare for the birth of Jesus. They also think of Jesus's promised second coming in the future.
- Advent is a time of great expectation and careful preparation. Advent customs, such as the Advent wreath, Advent candle and Advent calendar, take place in church and at home. They help Christians to focus on the true meaning of Christmas.

Christmas

Key terms

Incarnation God becoming fully human in Jesus Christ

Messiah the Hebrew name for the promised leader sent by God ('Christ' is the same word in Greek)

Christmas is the celebration of the birth of Jesus Christ. For most Christians, the Festival of Christmas begins on 25 December and lasts for twelve days. Orthodox Christians celebrate Christmas on 6 January, the date on which other Christians celebrate the festival of Epiphany (see pages 94–5).

The birth of Jesus

The account of Jesus's birth, or nativity, can be found in the gospels of Matthew and Luke. Their narratives show that Jesus was special from his conception and that God was present from the beginning. The gospel writers believed that Jesus was the **Messiah**, and that his birth was a tremendous moment in history. It was the point at which God's salvation began.

Luke in his gospel (2: 1–20) gives a more detailed account of the birth of Jesus. He describes how Caesar Augustus called a census of the Roman Empire, which demanded that people went to their own town to register. Joseph had to go from Nazareth in Galilee to Bethlehem in Judea, the town of David, because he was a descendant of David. He took with him Mary, who was pledged to be married to him. Mary was pregnant. While they were in Bethlehem she gave birth to her son, Jesus. She wrapped him in bands of cloth and placed him in a manger (an animal feeding trough), because there was no room at the inn.

That night an **angel** appeared to shepherds in the fields who were keeping watch over their flocks nearby. The angel told them not to be afraid since he had great news for them. The Messiah had been born in Bethlehem and they would find him wrapped in cloths, lying in a manger. Other angels appeared praising God – 'Glory to God on high, and on earth peace to men on whom his favour rests.'

When the angels left them, the shepherds decided go to Bethlehem to see the child. They found Mary, Joseph and the baby in the manger.

The importance of Jesus's birth

Christians believe that Jesus is God the Son. They also believe that he has always existed with the Father. The infant Jesus was God the Son taking on the nature of a human being. In him, God took on all that it means to be human. Christians call this event the **incarnation** – they believe that God came in flesh to the world. The beginning of John's Gospel emphasizes this belief.

> In the beginning was the Word, and the Word was with God, and the Word was God. He was with God in the beginning. The Word became flesh and made his dwelling among us. We have seen his glory, the glory of the One and Only, who came from the Father, full of grace and truth. (John 1: 1–2, 14)

Christians believe that Jesus was born of a virgin mother by the power of the Holy Spirit. He did not have a human father. Mary was told of her pregnancy by the angel Gabriel.

> The Holy Spirit will come upon you, and the power of the Most High will overshadow you. So the holy one to be born will be called the Son of God. (Luke 1: 35)

Christians see great significance in the manner of Jesus's birth. They point out that the Son of God was not born in a royal palace but in a stable. His first visitors were not great leaders, but shepherds. Christians believe this shows the universal nature of Jesus – he is the Saviour of the world.

Christians look upon the birth of Jesus as a sign of God's great love for humanity. This is the reason why Christians celebrate Christmas so joyfully. For Christians, Christmas marks the moment in time when God became man in Jesus Christ.

Inside the Church of the Nativity, Bethlehem. The star marks the spot where it is said Jesus was born.

The crib

One of the customs of the Advent and Christmas season is the display of a crib. A crib is a model of the stable where Jesus was born. It is a focal point of prayer and worship in church and at home. It was originally used by St Francis to teach people about the birth of Jesus. Today, cribs can be found in many churches and Christian homes during Advent, Christmas and Epiphany (see pages 92–5).

The crib contains the figures of Mary, Joseph, the shepherds and stable animals. It is customary to place the figure of the infant Jesus in the manger on Christmas Eve. Twelve days later, at Epiphany, the figures of the Wise Men are added.

Activities

1 In the Apostles' Creed, Christians state that Jesus was 'conceived by the power of the Holy Spirit and born of the Virgin Mary'. How important is it to believe that Jesus's conception and birth were special? Give reasons for your answer. **PS 2.1**

2 Hot seat activity: read the account of the announcement of Jesus' forthcoming birth to Joseph in Matthew 1: 18–25. One student takes on the role of Joseph. Students question him about his reaction to the news that the Holy Spirit has caused Mary to conceive. **C 2.1a, 2.2b, WO 2.1, 2.2**

Key points

- During the Festival of Christmas Christians celebrate the birth of Jesus Christ.
- Christians believe that God the Son became a man and lived on earth.
- Christians believe that Jesus was born of a virgin mother by the power of the Holy Spirit.

A crib scene on Christmas Day and at Epiphany.

A crib scene on Christmas Eve.

As well as the Advent wreath, Advent candle and Advent calendar, there are a number of other customs that remind Christians of the true meaning of Advent and Christmas.

Light

Light is an important symbol during Advent and Christmas. Jesus called himself the 'Light of the World' (John 8: 12) and light is used to welcome his coming. A number of customs at this time of the year involve the use of light, usually in the form of candles (see pages 88–9).

Light brings warmth, comfort and pleasure. It also illuminates things we would prefer remained hidden. In the same way, the symbol of light during Advent and Christmas represents the salvation and judgement Jesus brings at his coming.

Christingle

Several customs during Advent and Christmas are designed to help children understand the meaning of the birth of Christ. One of them is the Christingle.

A Christingle is an orange with a red ribbon around it. A small candle is set in the top. Four sticks, usually cocktail sticks, are placed in the orange. Pieces of fruit or small sweets are placed on the sticks.

A Christingle is full of symbolism. The orange represents the world. The red ribbon is the blood of Jesus shed for everyone at his crucifixion. The candle represents Jesus, the Light of the World. The four sticks are either the four seasons or the four corners of the world. The fruit and sweets represent the food that God provides.

Many churches hold Christingle services during Advent. Children are given a Christingle. In return, they may give an envelope containing money for a charity. The candles on the Christingles are lit during the service and the lights in the church are switched off. At this point a carol may be sung. The symbolism of the Christingle is explained to the congregation.

A Christingle is a symbol of the love of God and of Jesus, the Light of the World.

The Jesse Tree

The Jesse Tree is a popular Advent custom in many Christian homes. It is a bare branch, often sprayed silver or gold, set in a pot. Sometimes a small Christmas tree is used. It is used to show the ancestors of Jesus and events in the Bible from creation to the birth of Jesus.

Jesse was the father of King David. In the Old Testament there is a passage that many people believe prophesies that the Messiah will be a descendant of Jesse and David. The Jesse Tree is a symbol of this prophecy.

> A shoot will come up from the stump of Jesse;
> from his roots a Branch will bear fruit.
> (Isaiah 11: 1)

During Advent, the Jesse Tree is decorated with symbols of the ancestors of Jesus and of important events in the Bible. Often children design their own symbols on pieces of card, which are then hung on the branches. There are no set patterns to follow – children are encouraged to use their imagination. For example, Noah may be represented by an ark or a rainbow, Joseph by a coloured coat or a pyramid, Moses by a red letter C with a gap in the middle of the letter, Jesus by a manger, the shepherds by a lamb or a crook and the Wise Men by gifts or a star.

Symbols of Jesus' ancestors and Bible stories are hung on the Jesse Tree during Advent.

In many Christian homes, a symbol is hung on the Jesse Tree each day during Advent. Sometimes the Bible passage associated with the symbol is read. As with the Advent calendar (see page 89), the Jesse Tree can be used to guide Christians' preparations for celebrating the birth of Jesus.

Carol singing

Carol singing is a common custom during the Christmas season. Many Christians form groups and go from house to house singing carols. The words of the carols help to pass on the message of Christmas to others. Christians give the money raised from their carol singing to a charity.

Christmas presents and cards

Many Christians give presents to friends and family at Christmas. Christmas is a time of giving and receiving. This custom represents the gifts of the Wise Men to Jesus and God's gift of his Son, the greatest gift of all. For this reason some Christians prefer to exchange presents on 6 January, the festival of Epiphany (see pages 94–5).

Christians also send Christmas cards, perhaps with a religious picture and a Christian message.

Services during Advent and Christmas

Carol services are held during Advent and Christmas. Passages from the Bible, relating to the nativity, are read and carols are sung. Many congregations enjoy a service of Nine Lessons and Carols on the Sunday before Christmas Day. Other services during Advent

may include the Blessing of the Crib and toy services, when toys and games are donated to children in need.

A service of Midnight Mass is held in many Roman Catholic and Anglican churches. The service usually begins at 11.30 pm on Christmas Eve. During Midnight Mass all the carols, prayers and readings relate to the birth of Jesus. The figure of the infant Jesus may be placed in the crib at this time, and the communion will take place once midnight has passed. Many Christians enjoy welcoming the day of Christ's birth in this way.

There will be several services during the morning of Christmas Day. One of them may be a family service; another, a service of the Eucharist. Most Christians believe that it is important to join together to worship God on Christmas Day.

Activities

1 In groups, make a Jesse Tree. Choose a number of characters and important events from the Old Testament. Each member of the group should design a symbol on a small piece of card to represent the character or event they have chosen. **PS 2.1, 2.2, WO 2.1, 2.2, 2.3**

2 Discover more about customs used during Advent and Christmas by visiting the following websites:
www.soon.org.uk/christmas.htm
www.wickham.newbury.sch.uk/xmas/xmas tory.html and www.german-way.com
Choose two customs described there, then add the information given to your notes on Advent and Christmas customs. **IT 2.1, 2.2, 2.3**

Key points

- Customs during Advent and Christmas enable Christians to focus on the importance of the birth of Jesus.
- A number of customs, such as the Jesse Tree and the crib, help Christian families to prepare for and celebrate the birth of Jesus together in their own homes.

Epiphany

The Greek word *epiphany* means 'appearance' or 'showing'. It is the appearance of Jesus as God the Son to the world.

Epiphany is on 6 January. Christians think of the showing of Jesus to the world and of events such as the baptism of Jesus and his first teaching and miracles. The first of these events, the one most associated with the feast of Epiphany itself, is the showing of Jesus to the **Magi** (Wise Men).

The Wise Men

According to the Gospel of Matthew, the Wise Men followed a star from their homes in eastern countries to the town of Bethlehem. Although they would have been regarded as important men in their own right, they came not only to find a baby but also to worship him and present him with precious gifts. Read more about them in Matthew 2: 1–12.

There are a number of important points to note about the Wise Men.

- There is no mention of the number of Wise Men who visited Jesus. However, there is mention of three gifts – gold, frankincense and myrrh. This is probably the basis of the tradition that there were three visitors.

- The Wise Men were not present to worship the infant Jesus on the night of his birth. For this reason, the figures of the Wise Men are not placed in the crib scene until after the twelve days of Christmas (see page 91).

- Christians look upon the Wise Men's gifts as being symbolic. The gift of gold is a recognition of Jesus' kingship. Frankincense – used in prayer and worship – is a sign of Jesus's divinity. Myrrh – used to embalm the body after death – is a symbol of Jesus's future sacrifice.

- The Wise Men were **Gentiles** – they were not Jews. Their visit to Jesus marks the moment when God the Son was shown to the world. Epiphany is sometimes called the 'Feast of the Manifestation'.

Epiphany customs

In some parts of the world, January 6 is the day on which Jesus's birth is celebrated and gifts are exchanged. Orthodox Christians, in particular, follow this practice. Customs during Epiphany reflect the importance Christians place on the visit of the Wise Men to Jesus.

Caspar, Melchior and Balthasar

Traditionally, the Magi are called Caspar, Melchior and Balthasar, although there is no evidence to support this in the Bible. In a number of European countries, particularly Austria, Germany and Poland, pieces of chalk are blessed during the Epiphany service on 6 January. On returning home, families chalk the letters CMB, the year and a cross on the frame of their front door. The letters CMB may stand for the traditional names of the Magi. They may also be the first letters of the phrase, 'Christus Mansionem Benedicat', meaning 'Christ bless this house'. The chalk design is to show that there are Christians living in the house, and that the house will be Christ's for the rest of the year. This design can also be found on the doorframes of houses in Britain (for example, in Walsingham).

Carol singing

In Germany there is the custom of the 'Star Singers', particularly among members of the Roman Catholic tradition. Children dressed as the Wise Men and carrying a large star go from house to house singing Epiphany carols. They are given money to contribute towards a national charity, which changes from year to year.

Here is an Epiphany carol.

Wise Men, they came to look for wisdom,
finding one wiser than they knew;
rich men, they met with one yet richer –
King of the kings, they knelt to you:
Jesus our wisdom from above,
wealth and redemption, life and love.

Guests of their God, they opened treasures,
incense and gold and solemn myrrh,
welcoming one too young to question
how came these gifts, and what they were,
Gift beyond price of gold or gem,
make among us your Bethlehem.
(Christopher Idle, *Hymns for Today's Church*,
Jubilate Hymns)

Activities

1 Read the following first lines of *The Journey of the Magi*, a poem by T S Eliot.

A cold coming we had of it,
Just the worst time of the year
For a journey, and such a long journey:
The ways deep and the weather sharp,
The very dead of winter.

Ask your teacher for a copy of the full poem and read it carefully.

a In groups, produce a dramatic interpretation of the poem incorporating any or all of the following: reading, music, dance and mime.

b Having performed the interpretations in groups for the whole class, discuss the way you think the Wise Men would have felt during their journey.
C 2.1a, 2.1b, PS 2.1, 2.2, 2.3, WO 2.1, 2.2, 2.3

2 As Christians celebrate the coming of the Wise Men, they remember that the Christian faith is for people of every race and nation. Many Christians believe God is calling them to work with Christians in other countries. Visit a website that offers opportunities to share in such work, for example, www.methodist.org.uk/getinvolved/service.htm and www.tearfund.org **IT 2.1**

Key points

- The word 'epiphany' means 'appearance' or 'showing'. The festival begins on 6 January and ends on the day before Lent.
- At Epiphany, Christians think of the visit of the Magi (Wise Men) to Jesus. As the Magi were Gentiles, the festival celebrates the showing of Jesus to the world.
- Customs, such as chalking CMB on doorposts and Epiphany carol singing, show the importance Christians place on the visit of the Magi to Jesus.

Exam tips and practice questions

Below are some sample exam questions about Advent, Christmas and Epiphany. Questions **1** to **3** include examiner's tips to give you hints on how to score full marks. Questions **4** and **5** are for you to try on your own.

1 Describe two Christian customs used during the season of Advent. Show how the customs you have chosen help Christians prepare for the festival of Christmas. *(8 marks)*

2 Which figures would you find in a crib at Epiphany? Why would you expect to find them there? *(3 marks)*

3 'To keep Christmas special, all shops should be closed on Christmas Day.' Do you agree with this statement? Give reasons for your answer, showing that you have considered more than one point of view. *(5 marks)*

Try to answer the following questions on your own. Before you write your responses, think about your own hints on how to score full marks.

4 Describe a Christian service during either Advent or Christmas. State a tradition in which the service is likely to take place. *(4 marks)*

5 Do you think Christmas has become too commercialized? Give reasons for your answer, showing you have considered more than one point of view. *(5 marks)*

How to score full marks

The examiner would be marking on the basis of levels of response (see page vi), so make sure your responses are full and accurate.

1 This is a question to test what you know. Make sure you describe each custom clearly. You need also to include the purpose behind both customs, relating it to either Advent or Christmas. If you are not sure of the answer, pages 92–3 should help you.

2 This is a question to test your knowledge and understanding. You should refer to events in the Bible relating to the birth of Jesus to gain full marks.

3 This is an evaluation question to make you think and to test how well you can assess a problem or situation. Look for arguments for and against the statement you have to discuss. No more than three marks would be given to a response that only looks at one side of the question.

The Easter cycle of festivals

This section includes:

- Lent
- Palm Sunday
- Maundy Thursday
- Christian beliefs about the death of Jesus
- Good Friday
- Christian beliefs about the resurrection
- Easter
- Ascension and Pentecost.

The section includes units on what Christians believe about the death and resurrection of Jesus.

Lent is a time of preparation for Easter. It is a time of self-discipline for Christians. The last week of Lent is Holy Week, during which Christians think about the events from when Jesus rode into Jerusalem on Palm Sunday to his crucifixion.

Easter is the time when Christians celebrate the resurrection of Jesus. Forty days after the resurrection, on Ascension Day, Christians celebrate Jesus' return to the Father in heaven. Ten days later comes Pentecost or Whitsun, when they remember the coming of the Holy Spirit to the Church.

Lent

Key terms

Easter the celebration of the resurrection of Jesus

Lent the time of preparation for Easter

The Easter cycle of festivals

The festivals and holy days centred on Christmas relate to a fixed date, 25 December. The date of **Easter** changes from year to year. This is because Jesus died and rose at the time of the Jewish Passover festival, which is related to the time of the full moon. The earliest date is 22 March and the latest is 25 April.

Whatever the date of Easter, a range of dates moves forward and back through the calendar with it. This is because these festivals and other special days relate to events in the life of Jesus as an adult and to the coming of the Holy Spirit to the first Christians on the day of **Pentecost**.

Some Christians mark these special days with ceremonies to bring out the particular meaning of each day. Other Christians pay less attention to them.

The first of these dates is Ash Wednesday, the first day of **Lent**. Lent is the period of six and a half weeks leading up to Easter (40 days, not counting the Sundays).

It is the time for Christians to prepare themselves spiritually for the celebration of Easter. The word 'Lent' comes from the Old English word *Lencten*, meaning 'Spring'.

The table below shows how these special days vary from year to year. Note that in the Orthodox Churches the dates are sometimes different from the ones given here.

Jesus tempted

Matthew and Luke record in their gospels that Jesus spent 40 days in the desert. During these 40 days he prayed and fasted. While there, he was tempted or put to the test by the devil. But he did not give way to these temptations.

Lent is the time when Christians remember the temptations of Jesus. As a sign that they are focusing on Jesus' time in the desert, the season of Lent lasts 40 days. Sundays are not counted in reckoning the days, but – apart from Mid-Lent (Mothering) Sunday – Lent rules are observed every day.

Christians remember their own temptations. They remember how often they themselves have sinned. It is a time for **repentance** – feeling genuinely sorry for their sins and asking God's forgiveness.

Dates of Easter festivals and holy days, 2000–2011

Year	Ash Wednesday	Palm Sunday	Good Friday	Easter Day	Pentecost (Whitsun)
2000	8 March	16 April	21 April	23 April	11 June
2001	28 February	8 April	13 April	15 April	3 June
2002	13 February	24 March	29 March	31 March	19 May
2003	5 March	13 April	18 April	20 April	8 June
2004	25 February	4 April	9 April	11 April	30 May
2005	9 February	20 March	25 March	27 March	15 May
2006	1 March	9 April	14 April	16 April	4 June
2007	21 February	1 April	6 April	8 April	27 May
2008	6 February	16 March	21 March	23 March	11 May
2009	25 February	5 April	10 April	12 April	31 May
2010	17 February	28 March	2 April	4 April	23 May
2011	9 March	17 April	22 April	24 April	12 June

In many churches there are no flowers during Lent, a sign that this is a solemn time. In contrast, the churches are lavishly decorated to celebrate the joy of Easter.

Some Christians, especially Roman Catholics, prepare for Lent through the Sacrament of Reconciliation or **Penance**. In the presence of a priest they express their sorrow for their sin and ask God's forgiveness. The priest **absolves** them (pronounces God's forgiveness). An old English word for 'absolve' is shrive. The day before Lent begins is called Shrove Tuesday, since that is the day when many come to be shriven.

Making a Lent rule

While the 40 days of Lent do relate to the 40 days Jesus spent in the desert, it is primarily a time of preparation for Easter. As part of their preparation, Christians of many traditions make Lent rules. These rules are intended to help them develop a closer relationship with God through their self-discipline. A Lent rule has one or more parts to it.

- Giving up something that is innocent or harmless in itself as a self-discipline. An example might be eating sweets or biscuits, or having sugar in tea. By giving up sweets, a person may save some money. That money is given to a charity or other good cause.
- Giving up a sin or bad habit. Someone who swears or who is guilty of loss of temper may make a point of trying to get rid of the habit. This part of the rule may be helped by the first part. Every time a person thinks, 'I'd like a sweet', the next thought will be, 'It's Lent. I've given up sweets – and losing my temper!'
- Giving more time to spiritual things. Many churches run special courses during Lent. Some people make a point of being more regular in Sunday worship during Lent.

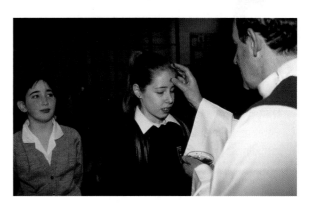

Ash Wednesday

The first day of Lent is called Ash Wednesday. The day gets its name from a ceremony performed on that day in Roman Catholic and some Anglican churches.

The priest makes the sign of the cross in ash on the forehead of each worshipper, at the same time saying, 'Remember you are dust and to dust you shall return. Turn away from evil and follow Christ.'

The Ash Wednesday rite is based on Old Testament symbols of repentance, 'Sackcloth and ashes'. The ash is traditionally made by burning some of the palm crosses from the previous year.

Activities

1. What is temptation? Why is it difficult to resist temptation? **PS 2.1**
2. Do you think self-discipline is an important part of a religion? If so, what do you think it achieves? Give reasons for your answer. **PS 2.1**

Key points

- Lent is the time of preparation for Easter.
- The 40 days of Lent remind Christians of the temptations of Jesus.
- During Lent Christians discipline themselves as a sign of repentance and to deepen their spiritual lives.
- Ash Wednesday, the first day of Lent, gets its name from a ceremony practised on that day.

Palm Sunday

Holy Week

The last week of Lent is called **Holy Week**. During Holy Week Christians recall those events in the life of Jesus that occurred in the days leading to his death and burial. In some churches those events are marked by special ceremonies to remind the worshippers of what happened and why.

Important days in Holy Week are:

- Palm (Passion) Sunday
- Maundy (Holy) Thursday
- Good Friday
- Holy Saturday.

Palm Sunday

Palm Sunday is also known as Passion Sunday by Roman Catholics. It celebrates the day when Jesus rode into Jerusalem on a donkey.

As Jesus and his disciples approached Jerusalem and came to Bethphage on the Mount of Olives, Jesus sent two disciples, saying to them, 'Go to the village ahead of you, and at once you will find a donkey tied there, with her colt by her. Untie them and bring them to me. If anyone says anything to you, tell him that the Lord needs them, and he will send them right away.' This took place to fulfil what was spoken through the prophet: 'Say to the Daughter of Zion, "See, your king comes to you, gentle and riding on a donkey, on a colt, the foal of a donkey."' The disciples went and did as Jesus had instructed them. They brought the donkey and the colt, placed their cloaks on them, and Jesus sat on them. A very large crowd spread their cloaks on the road, while others cut branches from the trees and spread them on the road. The crowds that went ahead of him and those that followed shouted,

A Palm Sunday procession on the Mount of Olives.

'Hosanna to the Son of David!' 'Blessed is he who comes in the name of the Lord!' 'Hosanna in the highest!' When Jesus entered Jerusalem, the whole city was stirred and asked, 'Who is this?' The crowds answered, 'This is Jesus, the prophet from Nazareth in Galilee.'
(Matthew 21: 1–11)

A decisive event

Jesus' entry into Jerusalem riding on a donkey is full of significance for Christians.

- The people were hoping and waiting for God to send them a leader, the Messiah. The Messiah would be descended from David, a great king who had lived 1000 years earlier. Old Testament prophets had written about the Messiah. One of them, Zechariah, had said, 'Your king comes to you, gentle and riding on a donkey.'
- Various people over the years had claimed to be the Messiah. Usually they were political leaders, wanting to overthrow the government. At the time of Jesus, government meant the Roman governor and his soldiers.
- Jesus' teaching was new and challenging. His miracles were a sign that he had unique power. People had been asking, 'Who is he? Can he be the Messiah?'

- Because Jesus' teaching was new and challenging, the religious leaders saw him as a threat. The last thing they wanted was to have people thinking that Jesus was the Messiah, a leader sent from God.
- When Jesus rode into Jerusalem on a donkey, he was saying, by his actions, 'I am the Messiah.' The people got the message and gave him a great welcome.
- 'Hosanna', they shouted. Hosanna is a Hebrew word meaning 'Save now'. When it appears in the Old Testament it is a shout of welcome to a great leader or even to God himself.
- 'Son of David' they called out to Jesus. This title means 'Messiah'.
- A great leader would ride into a city with carpets laid before him and would be welcomed with flowers and garlands. There was no time to lay on that sort of welcome, so people laid clothes on the ground or used leaves and branches from the nearby palm trees.
- By riding into Jerusalem, Jesus challenged the religious leaders in a way they could not ignore. He knew that they would try to kill him. He was going deliberately to his death.

Palm crosses and branches

The most common symbol of Palm Sunday is a palm cross. A leaf is taken from a palm branch and folded into the shape of a cross. In some cases, the crosses are made by African Christians – the money paid gives them an income and helps to provide important facilities for their community.

Palm crosses are given to worshippers on Palm Sunday. People hold them as the Palm Sunday gospel is read, a passage (such as Matthew 21: 1–11) describing the ride into Jerusalem. People take the crosses home. Often they keep them in their homes, perhaps attached to a cross or crucifix, or a religious picture. The palm leaf represents the way in which Jesus was welcomed as Messiah. The cross shape looks ahead to Good Friday and the crucifixion (see pages 106–7). On Palm Sunday Jesus went to Jerusalem knowing he was going towards his crucifixion.

A palm cross.

In some churches, palm branches are used. They are fastened to crosses in the church or are carried in processions. The processions may go outside the church and into the nearby streets. In a few places, a donkey may walk in the procession.

Activities

1. Hot seat activity: in turn, members of the class take the roles of different people who saw Jesus ride into Jerusalem, for example, disciples of Jesus, bystanders, religious leaders and Roman soldiers. The rest of the group act as journalists at a press conference and ask them about what happened. **C 2.1a, 2.1b**

2. If your local church made a Palm Sunday procession (with palm branches and perhaps even a donkey), what do you think the effect would be? **PS 2.1**

Key points

- During Holy Week, especially on particular days, Christians remember the suffering and death of Jesus.
- On Palm Sunday Christians remember how and why Jesus rode into Jerusalem on a donkey.
- Palm Sunday is observed by distributing palm crosses and by processions.

Maundy Thursday, also known as Holy Thursday, recalls how, on the night before he was crucified, Jesus and his disciples shared what is known as the Last Supper.

> The Lord Jesus, on the night he was betrayed, took bread, and when he had given thanks, he broke it and said, 'This is my body, which is for you; do this in remembrance of me.' In the same way, after supper he took the cup, saying, 'This cup is the new covenant in my blood; do this, whenever you drink it, in remembrance of me.' (1 Corinthians 11: 23–5)

With these words, Paul told the Christians in Corinth to celebrate the Holy Communion in remembrance of Jesus. Christians have done so ever since. (See also pages 42–9 on the Holy Communion.)

The Last Supper is specially remembered at the Eucharist on Maundy Thursday, since it was on that day, the day before he was crucified, that Jesus and his disciples met to eat the Passover.

The Passover meal

Over 1200 years before the time of Jesus, the Israelites (ancestors of the Jews) were slaves in Egypt. The Old Testament gives an account of how they escaped from slavery when Moses was chosen by God to lead them out of Egypt. By a series of remarkable events the people escaped through the Red Sea to Mount Sinai. There they made a covenant (binding promise) with God. He had saved them from slavery – they were to be his people and he would be their God.

A crucial event in the escape from Egypt was the last of ten plagues. The Israelites were told to kill lambs for a meal and to sprinkle some of their blood on the doorposts of their houses. The lambs were a sacrifice, an offering to God. The angel of death 'passed over' the houses of the Israelites, but the firstborn son of Egyptian families died.

Ever since, Jews have celebrated the covenant between themselves and God at Passover (in Hebrew, 'Pesach') each year.

The new covenant

As Jesus gave the wine to the disciples to drink, he said, 'This is the new covenant in my blood.' The new covenant is between God and Christians. The sacrifice is Jesus himself. Jesus is called 'the Lamb of God' in a number of places in the New Testament.

The link between the old covenant and the new covenant is stressed strongly in the Maundy Thursday rite.

A new commandment

The name 'Maundy' comes from the Latin word *mandatum*, meaning 'commandment'. Just as the old covenant included the Ten Commandments, so Jesus gave his disciples a new commandment.

> A new command I give you: Love one another. As I have loved you, so you must love one another. By this all men will know that you are my disciples, if you love one another. (John 13: 34–5)

The washing of feet

The most distinctive Maundy ceremony is the one that recalls how Jesus washed the feet of his disciples.

> Jesus got up from the meal, took off his outer clothing, and wrapped a towel round his waist. After that, he poured water into a basin and began to wash his disciples' feet, drying them with the towel that was wrapped round him. (John 13: 4–5)

The ceremony of the feet washing symbolizes that Christians, like Jesus, should be willing to serve one another.

In Britain, the tradition of the monarch washing the feet of beggars has been replaced by the giving of the Royal Maundy money.

The washing of feet was a slave's task. It would have seemed very strange to the disciples that Jesus was washing their feet and Peter protested that he should not be doing it, but Jesus insisted. He did it to show the disciples that they should be ready to serve each other.

> Now that I, your Lord and Teacher, have washed your feet, you also should wash one another's feet. I have set you an example that you should do as I have done for you. (John 13: 14–15)

In Roman Catholic and some Anglican churches, the priest washes the feet of twelve members of the congregation. Each sits with one foot bare; the priest pours water over the foot and dries it with a towel.

The Mass of chrism

The Last Supper was a meal Jesus shared with the disciples. Among Roman Catholics and Anglicans this is a day when priests meet for a Eucharist at the cathedral with their bishop. The Roman Catholic priests concelebrate the Mass with the bishop – they all consecrate the bread and wine together. At the service, the bishop consecrates the holy oils that are used by the priests for anointing at baptism and confirmation, and for the anointing of the sick.

After the meal

When the Last Supper was over, Jesus and his disciples went to a place called Gethsemane, where Jesus prayed. While he was there soldiers sent by the chief priests came and arrested Jesus. His disciples ran away and left him.

On this day, in some churches, the altar is stripped of its covering and ornaments after the communion and left bare, symbolizing the way in which Jesus was deserted. Consecrated bread and wine, the body and blood of Christ, may be taken to a side chapel. There may be a Watch kept in the chapel where the consecrated bread and wine have been placed. People stay to pray in the chapel. People come at varying times, so that they are watching with Jesus and praying with him, as he asked the disciples to do in Gethsemane.

Activities

1   Do you think that the feet-washing ceremony is a good way of showing how Christians should treat each other? Give reasons for your answer. **PS 2.1**

2   Visit www.royalreport.com to learn more about the Royal Maundy and the ideas behind the ceremony. Also, using a search engine, look for information about other Maundy traditions. **IT 2.1, 2.2**

Key points

- Maundy Thursday is the day of the Last Supper, a Passover meal marking the old covenant.
- At the Last Supper, Jesus instituted the Eucharist, the celebration of the new covenant. He told them, 'Do this in remembrance of me.'
- The washing of feet is a rite showing how Jesus was prepared to serve his disciples and how he wanted them to serve one another.
- Jesus gave a new commandment: 'Love one another as I have loved you.'

Christian beliefs about the death of Jesus

Christians think of the death of Jesus as a great and wonderful mystery. They do not pretend they can fully understand why Jesus was crucified. They do believe that in some marvellous way the death of Jesus can save them from the effects of their sins and give them hope of being with God in heaven after they have died.

Jesus's enemies

The obvious answer to the question, 'Why did Jesus die?' is that his enemies plotted against him. They arranged that one of his disciples should betray him. They arrested him in the garden of Gethsemane. Jesus was helpless as the soldiers seized him and his disciples ran away. He was trapped into saying that he was the Son of God. They persuaded Pilate to sentence him to death. He was crucified.

On one level, that is the answer. But for Christians that is only a small part of the answer. Christians today believe that Jesus died because he chose to die for the sins of the world.

Jesus knew he would die

Jesus told his disciples a number of times that he was going to die and rise again. The disciples did not grasp what he meant. Each time he talked about his coming death, he spoke of himself as the Son of Man. The Son of Man was the heavenly figure referred to in the Book of Daniel. Whenever Jesus used the title Son of Man, it was with a sense of his own unique destiny.

> He said to them, 'The Son of Man is going to be betrayed into the hands of men. They will kill him, and after three days he will rise.'

But they did not understand what he meant and were afraid to ask him about it.
(Mark 9: 31–2)

Jesus went deliberately to his death

Jesus could have avoided his arrest and death. In many ways he seemed to go deliberately towards his crucifixion.

- He went to Jerusalem knowing what would happen when he got there. His disciples were uneasy about going, but Jesus went forward, telling the disciples about what was to come but going to Jerusalem regardless.

- Jesus rode into Jerusalem on a donkey. By entering Jerusalem in this way he showed that he claimed to be the Messiah (see pages 100–1).

- At the Last Supper Jesus knew that Judas was going to betray him, but he did not try to stop him.

- Jesus knew that Judas would bring the soldiers to Gethsemane, but he went to pray there just the same.

- Jesus did not try to prove his innocence, even though Pilate seemed to be on his side.

The Son of Man gave his life

Jesus said, 'The Son of Man did not come to be served, but to serve, and to give his life as a ransom for many.' He meant that his death in some way took away the punishment deserved by sinners because of the sins of which they were guilty.

Christians define sin as disobeying the will of God. When people sin, they are breaking God's law. Sin separates the human race from God. By sinning, humans set up a barrier between themselves and God.

Jesus gave his life to remove that barrier. Christians believe that the death of Jesus was a ransom that, in a sense, paid the price of sin.

Jesus's death was a sacrifice

In the Old Testament law, people were told to offer certain **sacrifices** to God. In particular, on the **Day of Atonement** they were to offer special sacrifices to pray for God's forgiveness. One such offering was the scapegoat, the goat that was sent off into the wilderness bearing away the sins of the people.

The offerings in the Old Testament law had to be offered year by year. Christians believe that Jesus's death was the perfect sacrifice, offered to God, to reconcile the human race to Him. They believe the sacrifice was complete and never needs to be repeated.

God gave his only son

Christians believe in God as a loving father. It was because of God's love for the human race that Jesus was born, died and rose again. Jesus took the step that would allow people to be forgiven and to be close to God.

The meaning of Jesus' death

Christians believe that their relationship with God depends on the death and resurrection of Jesus. Without the death of Jesus, humans have no chance of being close to God or of obtaining forgiveness from their sins.

Christians must accept for themselves the benefits of Jesus's death. There has to be a response to the love of God. Individual Christians must accept Jesus as a personal Saviour and Lord.

Christians believe that in baptism they are baptized into the death of Jesus (see pages 64–5). They remember the words of Paul in his letter to the Christians in Rome.

> Or don't you know that all of us who were baptized into Christ Jesus were baptized into his death? We were therefore buried with him through baptism into death in order that, just as Christ was raised from the dead through the glory of the Father, we too may live a new life. (Romans 6: 3–5)

Christians who baptize by total immersion believe that the immersion symbolizes dying to sin with Christ. The rising from the water symbolizes rising to new life with Jesus.

Salvador Dali's Christ of St John of the Cross, towering over the everyday world below.

Activities

1 Many people wear crosses and crucifixes. Why do they do so? Is it right for people who are not Christians to wear them? Give reasons for your answer. **PS 2.1**

2 Read the following passages about the death of Jesus.
 - John 3: 14–17.
 - Philippians 2: 5–11.

 What do these verses say about why Jesus died? **PS 2.1**

Key points

- The death of Jesus was a sacrifice freely made by him.
- Since Jesus's life was free from sin, his death is an offering that can take away the sins of the world.
- God's love for the human race is shown by his giving his son to die for their sins.
- Through baptism Christians share Jesus' risen life.

Good Friday

Key terms

Good Friday the day when Christians remember the crucifixion of Jesus

The cross

Jesus was put on trial by Pontius Pilate, the Roman governor, and sentenced to death. The soldiers mocked and abused him. He was made to carry his cross to a place outside the city walls of Jerusalem. There he was fastened to the cross. He hung there for many hours until he died.

Each of the four gospels describes the crucifixion in some detail. They describe things said and done by religious leaders, soldiers, disciples of Jesus and bystanders. They record seven times when Jesus himself spoke.

The crucifixion and resurrection of Jesus are the central events in the Christian faith. That is why **Good Friday** and Easter Day are such important days in the Christian year.

Why Good Friday?

You might wonder why Christians should call the day Good Friday when it was the day of Jesus's painful death. People explain this in two ways.

- The day is good because it was the best thing that could have happened for the world. The death of Jesus opens the way to heaven for everyone.
- The name is a corruption of God's Friday.

Focusing on the cross

The cross is the central theme of worship on Good Friday. The crucifixion is remembered in different churches in these and other ways.

- The account of what happened is read or acted in dramatic form. A team of readers or actors will take different parts.
- A large wooden cross is brought into the church. The congregation come one by one to kiss the foot of the cross as an act of devotion.

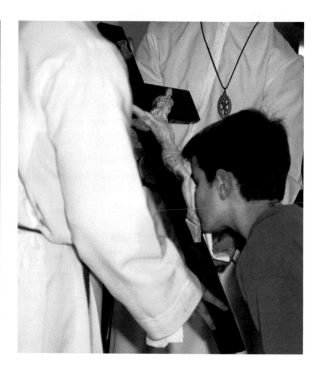

- In the gospels, it is stated that the area was plunged into darkness from twelve noon until three o'clock in the afternoon, the time when Jesus died. In some churches, there is a service covering those three hours, or at least the final hour. Hymns, prayers, readings and sermons all draw people's thoughts to the cross.

Communion on Good Friday

In many churches, there is no communion on Good Friday. The Lord has been taken away. Elsewhere, again because the Lord has been taken away, there is communion but no consecration. The consecrated bread and wine, which were taken to the side chapel on Maundy Thursday, are brought back and used for the Good Friday communion.

Processions of witness

In many places, Christians of different denominations join for a procession through a city or town. The procession passes through the streets, usually with one or two people carrying a large wooden cross, which may be placed in a square or other area large enough to allow a short act of worship to take place.

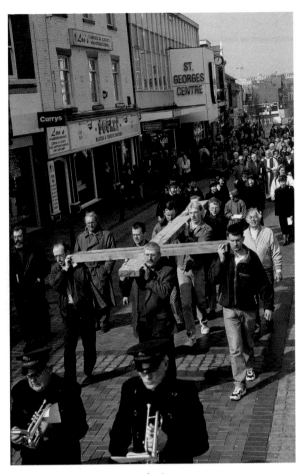

A Good Friday procession of witness.

Devotional drama for Good Friday.

The procession is an act of witness. It shows that the death of Jesus is an important event to Christians – important enough for them to want everyone to be conscious that it is Good Friday, the day of the crucifixion. The procession also shows that, whatever differences there may be between them, Christians all believe that Jesus died to save everyone who accepts him as Lord and follows him.

Good Friday evening

When Jesus died, some of his followers were allowed to take his body to be buried. One of them, Joseph of Arimathaea, owned a garden nearby, in which a tomb had already been prepared. Jesus' body was taken and placed in that tomb.

The Orthodox rite for Good Friday evening relates to the burial of Jesus. The central act of the rite is the bringing into the church of an icon of the dead Jesus wrapped in burial clothes. Members of the congregation come one by one to kiss the icon as an act of devotion.

Activities

1   In each of the gospels, read the accounts of the crucifixion and make a list of the things Jesus said while he was being crucified. **C 2.2, PS 2.1**

2   Make enquiries at churches in your area about things that happen there on Good Friday, such as acts of worship. Ask if there are any things that church members would *not* do on Good Friday. Why are these activities avoided on this day? **PS 2.1**

Key points

- Good Friday is the day when Christians remember the crucifixion of Jesus.
- On Good Friday worship includes reading the accounts of the death of Jesus.
- Good Friday is a day when Christians often worship together, sometimes with a procession through a town as a public act of witness.

The idea that Jesus died and then was alive once more is stated clearly in the gospels and in other books of the New Testament. In his letters, Paul makes it clear that Jesus did rise from the dead. In his first letter to the Corinthians, he gives a list of people who saw Jesus. The death, burial and resurrection of Jesus were the great events on which the whole Christian gospel was based.

For some people, it seems that belief in the resurrection has no place in the modern world. People do not rise from the dead. It cannot happen. If it cannot happen, then it did not happen.

It is important to remember that this is nothing new. Belief that Jesus rose from the dead has always been a problem for many people. Even in the New Testament, there are plenty of examples of people who found the whole idea of the resurrection simply incredible. Not even the disciples believed it at first.

The resurrection really happened

From the start, the resurrection was central to Christianity. The first Christians preached that Jesus had risen. They refused to give way and say it was not true – they were totally convinced. Paul was a case in point.

In Acts 26, Paul speaks to King Agrippa and the Roman governor, Festus. He tells how he became a Christian and they listen with interest. Paul finishes by saying, 'I am saying nothing beyond what the prophets and Moses said would happen – that the Christ would suffer and, as the first to rise from the dead, would proclaim light to his own people and to the Gentiles.' At this point Festus interrupted Paul. 'You are out of your mind, Paul!' he shouted. 'Your great learning is driving you insane.' Paul did not apologise. In reply he stated firmly once again his belief that Jesus had risen from the dead.

Like Paul, many Christians believe that Jesus physically rose from the dead. They also believe that after the resurrection the body of Jesus was in some way different. According to Luke and John, people who knew Jesus well did not recognize him at first. In 1 Corinthians 15, Paul talks of a physical body and a spiritual body.

The resurrection of the body

For all Christians the important thing about the resurrection of Jesus is that he is alive now. Death did not destroy him. He was a living spiritual reality to his followers, even after his crucifixion. They experienced his power and presence with them. In the same way, Christians today experience Jesus as a living spiritual power, present with them in their everyday lives.

Christians have varying views about what happened to the body of Jesus after the resurrection. To many Christians, the body of the risen Jesus was the same body as before. The wounds from the crucifixion were there in his hands, feet and side. But the body had been transformed. Jesus was able to come and go even when doors were shut. For example, John's Gospel reads:

> On the evening of that first day of the week, when the disciples were together, with the doors locked for fear of the Jews, Jesus came and stood among them and said, 'Peace be with you!' Yet Jesus was not a ghost. He told his disciples to touch him and be sure that he was really there. (John 20: 19)

Many Christians see a cross without a figure of Christ on it as showing that Jesus has risen from death.

The spiritual resurrection

Some Christians do not attach much importance to the physical aspect of the resurrection. They may find the idea difficult to understand. To them, the important aspect of the resurrection of Jesus is that he is alive and present with people today.

Christians holding such beliefs are sometimes accused of not believing that Jesus rose from the dead. Their attitude is that it does not matter whether the tomb was empty or whether Jesus returned to earth in a bodily form. If people find it difficult to believe in that sort of resurrection, there is no need for them to pretend to believe what they do not believe. What matters is that Jesus was and is really present. A person who believes that the risen Jesus is alive in the world today can be a true Christian.

'I am with you always'

The last words Jesus spoke in Matthew's Gospel are 'I am with you always, to the very end of the age.' The resurrection shows that Jesus is the Son of God. Christians rely on his promise that he will always be with them.

This crucifix shows the risen Jesus, the great High Priest in heaven.

- Christians feel they can pray to God at any time. They believe Jesus is with them, and that his death and resurrection make it possible for them to speak to God. They often pray 'through Jesus Christ, our Lord'.
- They believe that Jesus is truly present with them in the Eucharist. He is with them in his risen power. Many Christians believe that the bread and wine are the body and blood of Christ. It is the risen Jesus who is with them.
- Christians believe that wherever they are or whatever they are doing, Jesus is with them.

Easter

For Christians, Easter is the celebration of the resurrection, the greatest event in history. The resurrection was seen by nobody. In the gospels the first anyone knew about it was when the women went on the Sunday morning to the tomb. An angel was waiting for them. He told them that Jesus had risen.

The news was incredible. The followers of Jesus simply did not believe that he was alive. Only when they saw Jesus for themselves did the women and the disciples accept that it really had happened. Once they were convinced it was true, nothing would ever make them change their minds.

Every Sunday is a celebration of the resurrection. The reason that Christians celebrate Sunday as their holy day is that it was a Sunday when Jesus rose from the dead.

Christians celebrate Easter in many ways. Church buildings, stripped bare for Good Friday, are lavishly decorated with flowers. The worshippers sing joyful hymns, choruses and songs.

The new fire of Easter

No one saw Jesus rise from the dead. It had happened at some time during the night. Therefore, in many Roman Catholic, Orthodox and Anglican churches, the Easter Vigil is held to celebrate the resurrection of Jesus, the Light of the World. The service begins at a time when everywhere is dark.

It may begin after sunset on Holy Saturday, or at midnight, or perhaps before dawn on Easter Day itself. An important feature of the rite is the lighting of the new fire of Easter and the blessing and lighting of the paschal candle.

- Usually, the rite begins outside the church and in total darkness.
- A light is struck and the new fire of Easter is lit.
- The candle is blessed and lit from the new fire.
- The candle is carried through the church to the special stand where it is placed.
- The people in the congregation will have been given candles or tapers. As the candle is carried through the church, some light their own candles from it and pass the light along by lighting the candles of those near them. This symbolizes the spread throughout the world of the joyful news of the resurrection of Jesus.

The paschal candle

The paschal candle represents the risen Jesus.

A Greek Orthodox Easter sunrise service, welcoming the dawn of Easter Day.

The paschal candle is lit to represent the rising of Jesus, the Light of the World. The meaning of the symbols on the candle are as follows.

- The cross symbolizes the crucifixion.
- The five pieces of incense (or of brass) symbolize the wounds on Jesus' body – the crown of thorns, the nails in his hands and feet and the spear in his side.
- The Alpha (A) and Omega (Ω) represent Jesus, the beginning and end of all things.
- The numbers are those of the year.

The candle, a symbol of new life, is lit during the Easter season and then until Ascension (see page 112).

Easter gardens

In many churches at Easter you may find an Easter garden. This is a model of the tomb of Jesus set in a garden. The model in a large church or cathedral may be lifesize, or children may make small Easter gardens on plates or in small trays.

The tomb has a flat, round stone across the entrance. On Holy Saturday, when the body of Jesus was in the tomb, the entrance is closed with the stone. On Easter Day the stone is rolled back to show that the grave is empty. Inside is a piece of white cloth. In John's Gospel it is recorded that, when the disciples arrived at the tomb on the Sunday morning, they saw lying there the graveclothes in which Jesus had been wrapped.

Easter eggs

Eggs are popular symbols of Easter, and nowadays Easter eggs are usually made of chocolate. An egg looks lifeless – you can find stones that look like eggs. In the same way, the cave in which Jesus was buried looked lifeless, with the stone rolled across. But when an egg hatches, life springs from what seemed lifeless. In this way, an egg symbolizes the resurrection.

Red eggs are given to Orthodox Christians after the Easter Liturgy. They crack their eggs against each other's. The cracking of the eggs symbolizes a wish to break away from the bonds of sin and misery and enter the new life issuing from Christ's resurrection.

A traditional Easter exchange is, 'Christ is risen.' 'He is risen indeed. Alleluia.'

Activities

1 Visit this website: www.northerncross.co.uk. Read about the Easter pilgrimage to Holy Island (Lindisfarne). Imagine yourself taking part in the pilgrimage and write a diary of the events day by day.
C 2.3, IT 2.1, 2.2, PS 2.1, 2.2

2 Research the word 'Alleluia' (also spelt 'Hallelujah'). Where does it come from? What does it mean? When do Christians use the word and why? Make notes on your research. **PS 2.1**

Key points

- Easter celebrates Jesus rising from the dead.
- For Christians, the resurrection is the greatest event in history.
- Worship is full of joyful celebration at Easter. Many Christians decorate their churches.
- Christians use symbols, such as light and eggs, to show the meaning of resurrection.

Ascension and Pentecost

Ascension

The gospels record that during the 40 days after the resurrection Jesus appeared on a number of occasions to his followers. On one occasion, over 500 people saw him. At other times there were only one or two.

At the end of the 40 days, Jesus was with his disciples on the Mount of Olives. As he spoke to them for the last time, he went up from them until a cloud came across and they could see him no more. This event is called the ascension.

Christians do not celebrate the ascension just because it marks the end of Jesus' life on earth.

- At the ascension, Jesus returned to reign in glory with the Father.
- Jesus did not die again – he had destroyed the power of death through his crucifixion and resurrection. He is alive forever.
- Jesus was both divine and human. At the ascension, he returned to the Father with his human nature, as well as his divine nature.
- Jesus is ever interceding for the human family. Christians offer their prayers through him to the Father. Often they end prayers with words such as, 'through Jesus Christ our Lord.'

In the Apostles' Creed, Christians state their belief that after the resurrection Jesus ascended into heaven and is now once again with the Father.

Filled with the Holy Spirit

Ten days later Jerusalem was filled with pilgrims for the festival of **Pentecost**. Many were Jews who lived and worked in other countries and didn't speak Hebrew. They still thought of themselves as Jews. They kept to their Jewish religion. Jerusalem was still dear to them.

From many different countries, speaking many languages, they had come to the Holy City for the festival.

It was early – about nine o'clock – and many pilgrims were out walking. Suddenly a great commotion broke out in one part of the city. The crowd went to listen, curious to know what was happening.

The commotion was caused by the disciples. Jesus had told them to wait in Jerusalem and the Holy Spirit would come to them. Now they had received the Holy Spirit. They went out to preach the gospel.

> When the day of Pentecost had come, the disciples were all together in one place. And suddenly a sound came from heaven like the rush of a mighty wind, and it filled all the house where they were sitting. And there appeared to them tongues as of fire, distributed and resting on each one of them. And they were all filled with the Holy Spirit and began to speak in other tongues, as the Spirit gave them utterance. (Acts 2: 1–4)

Preaching the gospel

The crowd were fascinated and puzzled. 'What's happening?' asked some. 'They're drunk,' said others. Then Peter began to preach.

What an important time that was. The crowd was there, ready to listen. Peter had to get his message across clearly – there would be no second chance. He told them about Jesus Christ. He told them about his death and resurrection. He told them that Jesus was their Messiah and their Lord. The impact was dramatic.

> When the people heard this, they were cut to the heart and said to Peter and the other apostles, 'Brothers, what shall we do?' Peter replied, 'Repent and be baptized, every one of you, in the name of Jesus Christ for the forgiveness of your sins. And you will receive the gift of the Holy Spirit.' Those who accepted his message were baptized, and about three thousand were added to their number that day. (Acts 2: 37, 38, 41)

The Holy Spirit

At Pentecost, Christians are not only looking to the past, remembering that the Holy Spirit came to the apostles. They are also celebrating that the Holy Spirit has been with the Church ever since.

- It is important to Christians that the Holy Spirit is active in the Church. Many believe that he comes to them in a special way through certain sacraments, such as confirmation and ordination.

- It is important to them that the Holy Spirit is with them as individuals to guide and help them.

- No one can limit the power of the Holy Spirit. He comes to people without warning and in great power, as he did at Pentecost. Pentecostalists, as their name implies, believe strongly in the power of the Holy Spirit given in this way and filling their lives.

In John's Gospel, the Holy Spirit is likened to the wind, which is invisible and yet can be seen and felt. The Holy Spirit cannot be seen, but he affects the lives of those he touches (John 3: 8).

Paul wrote about the fruit of the Spirit, characteristics a Christian aims to adopt with the guidance of the Holy Spirit.

> The fruit of the Spirit is love, joy, peace, patience, kindness, goodness, faithfulness, gentleness and self-control. (Galatians 5: 22–3)

'Go and preach!'

Mark's Gospel records that, before Jesus left the disciples, he gave them the command 'Go into all the world and preach the good news to all creation' (Mark 16: 15). Acts chapter 2 describes how at Pentecost that preaching began.

Pentecost is sometimes called the Birthday of the Church. It was the day when, after Jesus had left them, his followers began to proclaim the gospel. They were no longer disciples, learners. They were apostles, sent out with a mission for the world.

Whitsun

Another name for Pentecost is Whitsun. It seems that the name comes from 'White Sunday'. One idea is that those baptized at Pentecost wore white robes; another that those baptized at Easter wore their white robes till Pentecost.

Whit walks are acts of witness, showing the onlookers that the Church is alive and active.

Activities

1. Thought-tracking activity: working in groups of three, take on the following roles: one student is Peter preaching on the day of Pentecost and the other two are onlookers. **C 2.1a, WO 2.1, 2.2**

2. Design a wall-hanging or stained-glass window to go inside a church to illustrate the power of the Holy Spirit. Note that white and red are colours strongly associated with the Holy Spirit. **PS 2.1, 2.2**

Key points

- On Ascension Day Christians celebrate Jesus' return to heaven, to reign in glory with the Father.

- They believe that Jesus is for ever interceding for the human race.

- Pentecost or Whitsun is the festival celebrating the coming of the Holy Spirit.

- Christians believe that the Holy Spirit has been present with Christians in the world ever since.

Exam tips and practice questions

Below are some sample exam questions about Lent, Holy Week, Easter and Pentecost. Questions **1** and **2** include examiner's tips to give you hints on how to score full marks. Questions **3** to **6** are for you to try on your own.

1 Choose two ceremonies that Christians use to mark holy days in Lent. Describe each and explain its meaning. *(10 marks)*

2 On some occasions, such as Good Friday and Pentecost, Christians take part in processions in town centres and other public places. Do you think such processions can be effective ways of spreading the Christian faith? Give reasons for your answer, showing you have considered more than one point of view. *(5 marks)*

Try to answer the following questions on your own. Before you write your responses, think about your own hints on how to score full marks.

3 a Name a day of the Christian year on which the altar is stripped of ornaments and coverings. *(1 mark)*

b Why is the altar left bare in this way? *(3 marks)*

4 Christians regard Lent as a time for preparing for Easter. In what ways are they preparing for Easter by the way they worship and live their lives during Lent? *(8 marks)*

5 Why is the resurrection of Jesus important to Christians today? *(6 marks)*

6 'A Christian can remember the death and resurrection of Jesus without special days and special ceremonies.' Do you agree with this statement? Give reasons for your answer, showing you have considered more than one point of view. *(5 marks)*

How to score full marks

1 This is a question to test what you know and understand. It would be marked on a point-by-point basis. First, note that the question is about holy days in Lent. Do not include ceremonies related to Easter or some other time in the Christian year. Describe each chosen ceremony carefully and explain it clearly. Check what you have written to make sure your answer is complete.

2 This is an evaluation question to make you think and to test your judgement. Make sure you consider more than one point of view – you will not score more than three marks if you do not. You should discuss the aims of those taking part in the act of witness, whether or not they are legitimate aims, and whether or not they are likely to be effective. You should also discuss the processions from the point of view of onlookers – some, but not all, of whom will be believers.

Coursework

Coursework is an essential part of the GCSE examination. You will have to produce one piece of coursework of 1000–1500 words on Christianity and 20 per cent of the total mark for the course is awarded for coursework.

In your coursework you will be assessed on the following.

- What you know about Christianity and how it has influenced what people believe and do (knowledge).
- Your ability to explain what Christians believe and how their beliefs affect the way they live and worship (understanding).
- Your ability to give a personal opinion, while showing you appreciate other points of view (evaluation).

As you will be marked separately on these three objectives, it is important that all three skills are shown.

Knowledge

It is not enough merely to gather as much information as you can. You need to show that you know what is really important. Look at the following example.

Task: Why is the role of Pope considered important by Roman Catholics?

Answer: The Pope is the leader of the Roman Catholic Church throughout the world. Roman Catholics believe that each Pope is a successor to St Peter, who was chosen by Jesus to be 'the rock' on whom the Church was to be built. They also believe that Peter was given special powers that are passed on to each Pope in the laying on of hands. When the Pope speaks 'ex cathedra' (or 'from the chair'), his pronouncements on faith or morals are thought by many to be infallible – without error. Roman Catholics believe that at such times the Pope and his bishops are guided by the Holy Spirit.

Each Pope is elected by the cardinals of the Roman Catholic Church from among their number. It is believed that the choice is inspired by the Holy Spirit. The Pope and the bishops together form the teaching authority of the Roman Catholic Church, called the magisterium. It is their responsibility to make sure that the teachings and actions of the Church remain faithful to the gospel of Jesus Christ. The Pope has the ultimate authority in this.

He represents Christ in the world and is thought by many, not just Roman Catholics, to have an important role to play as a world leader. He is particularly respected as a guide when dealing with the problems of modern living. Once elected, the Pope remains in this position for the rest of his life and has the ultimate responsibility for the spiritual welfare of all Roman Catholics.

Comment: This is a good answer. All the main points are concisely and clearly made. This part of the assignment is testing knowledge – the ability to select the right material and to present it accurately. The candidate has done this and also used a number of keys words, for example, cardinal, ex cathedra, infallible and magisterium. The candidate has shown understanding as well and would receive credit for doing so. The candidate has explained the historical background of the Pope's authority and has shown an understanding of the Pope's role in the world today.

When you have a choice of subject, make sure you choose someone or something about which there is enough to say. Read the question carefully. What is it about the thing you have chosen that answers the question? Make sure that everything is relevant there. At the same time, leave out anything that is not asked for.

Do not just copy out the words from, for example, the Bible or a prayer book. That does not show ability to select relevant material.

Understanding

You have shown what you know. Now you need to show that you understand. In fact, you have shown some understanding already. You show understanding by the way you select and comment on material. Now you must go further to show that you are aware of the significance of the information you have given. Make sure you know what the question is really asking. Look at this example.

> **Task:** Why do Christians use the Lord's Prayer?
>
> **Answer:** Christians use the Lord's Prayer because Jesus taught them the prayer and told them to use it. When the disciples said to Jesus, 'Lord teach us to pray,' he replied, 'When you pray, say …' and then he gave them the prayer. Another reason for using the prayer is that it contains many forms of Christian prayer. There is adoration ('For thine is the Kingdom, the power and the glory, for ever and ever. Amen'), confession ('Forgive us our trespasses') and petition ('Give us this day our daily bread'). The prayer is widely known and loved. It is used in both public and private worship. It is used by all Christians in worship and so represents the bond between them. In a crisis a person who is not used to prayer, but who knows the Lord's Prayer, may feel able to pray because he knows the words.
>
> **Comment:** This candidate has given a number of reasons for the importance of the Lord's Prayer. The candidate has shown understanding of what prayer is and why people pray. Different aspects of prayer have been recognized and examples given. Each example relates to one part or another of the prayer. The candidate has shown why this particular prayer is important to Christians by saying that the prayer was from Jesus himself.

You need to be able to show that you understand:

- the meaning of any words or actions you describe.
- the link between what Christians believe and what they do.
- the relationship between the life and teaching of Jesus and how Christians try to live their lives today.

When you make a statement showing understanding, make sure that you support your statement with an example or illustration.

Evaluation

You have shown what you know and understand. Now you need to give your opinion – to say what you think. You must show that you understand more than one point of view. In fact, you need not make a final judgement. You can simply give two or more points of view and say what you think is good or bad about each. Look at this example.

> **Task:** 'It is better to be baptized when you are older.' Do you agree?
>
> **Answer:** I think that people should be baptized when they are old enough to know what they are doing. They have come to know Jesus in a personal way and want to commit their lives to him. The decision to be baptized is theirs. Believers' baptism means exactly that – it is the baptism of believers, unlike infant baptism, where promises are made on behalf of the baby by parents and godparents. Believers' baptism is a way of showing others your love of God and that you want to follow a Christian way of life. Also in Mark 1: 9–11, we are told that Jesus was baptized when he was an adult. So I think that must be the best example to follow.
>
> But some Christians think that you should be baptized as a baby. This is because the child will become a member of the family of the Church at an early age. The child will grow up learning to love God with the help of the people in the church and the godparents. Some Christians think that as we are humans we are born into a sinful world and baptism cleans us from these sins. I also think that parents of sick babies find real comfort in knowing that their child has been baptized.
>
> **Comment:** This is a balanced answer. The candidate has given his own point of view based on good knowledge and understanding. It is quite a strong argument and the points are clearly made. The candidate has also given another point of view in a fair and balanced way.

It may not be his opinion, but his approach is positive – he does not criticize the beliefs of others. It is important in a question such as this to give more than one point of view. Full marks will not be given for answers that have only one point of view however good the answer is.

You will notice that when the stronger candidates quote from the Bible they give the reference (book, chapter, verses). You should always do the same when writing your assignments. See the section on gathering information below.

Writing your assignment

Before you start to write your assignment, make sure that you understand what you have to do. Read the title a number of times and try to see what the assignment is really about.

Gathering information

a Books will probably be your main source of information.
  - Make sure you can understand the books you use, otherwise what you write may be very muddled.
  - What you take from the books must be relevant to the topic.
  - Do not copy everything from the book word for word. You must show that you can understand what you are writing. Use your own words.
  - You can use short quotations when there is a good reason to do so, such as quoting a person's exact words or a passage from scripture. If you do, put the quotation in inverted commas and give the exact reference.
  - If you use a book, make a note of the title, author and publisher. You will need to list your sources on the coursework cover sheet.

b You may wish to make use of the Internet.
  - You will not receive any credit just because you have found something on the Internet. However, you will receive credit if you make good use of what you have found.
  - You must realize that, while some books are written as resource material for people doing coursework and other research, websites are not.
  - Much of what has been said about the use of books applies also to websites.
  - If you use a website, make a note of the name and address. You will need to list it among your sources on the coursework cover sheet.

c Interviews are an important way of getting information and opinions.
  - Be sure in your mind why you want to talk to this person and what you need to learn from the interview. Remember that the person to whom you are talking may not understand what you need to know.
  - Prepare carefully for the interview. Read about the subject first. Have a list of questions ready.
  - Take a tape recorder (and spare tapes) with you to record the conversation. Check that the person you are interviewing agrees to having the interview recorded.
  - Ask questions about the person's opinions to cover the evaluation aspect.

d The subject of your assignment may be suitable for a survey.
  - Make sure you understand what the survey is for. Do you wish to find out what people know or what they think? If you ask people 'What is prayer?' you are asking what they know. If you ask people 'Do you believe prayers are answered today?' you are asking what they think. Your survey can, of course, include both sorts of question.
  - Make sure you interview a reasonable number of people. If you ask too few, your survey will be too limited. If you ask too many, you will have too much information to include in your assignment. About 20–25 is a good number. Even so, make clear that you understand that this is a small sample. Among a sample of 20 people a majority may think that God does not answer prayer. A sample of 200 or 2000 may think otherwise.

- Try to ask people of different ages, backgrounds and gender. Remembering that this a religious studies assignment, try to have people of different denominations. Also try to get a mixture of people who are very committed to their faith, people who are not so committed and those who have no faith at all.

- Word the questions carefully. Give people a chance to say what they really think. For example, imagine you are writing an assignment on the Virgin Mary. You might include the question, 'Do you think Mary is a good role model for modern Christians?' If you ask the question, 'Can you think of ways in which Mary is a good role model for modern Christians?' you are letting people say what they really think. Listen to their answers and write them down carefully.

- Once you have completed your survey, try to analyse the information and the opinions you have been given. For example, do young people's views differ from older people's? Do the views of males differ from the views of females? If there are differences, why do you think that is?

- If you can, use a diagram, chart or graph to show what the figures mean.

e   What you can find out for yourself is important. If there is something local that is anything to do with your assignment, go and look at it for yourself. Take some photographs. Note carefully what you see and hear. Remember that you must ask permission first.

After gathering your information

- Before you start writing, read the assignment title again.
- Have you enough information to answer all parts of the question? Check each part to make sure.
- If you are not sure about anything in the title, or what you have to do, ask your teacher.
- Make sure that everything you are going to use is relevant to the question. If it is not relevant, do not use it, however interesting it may be. Such material will gain you no marks.

Preparing to write

- Remember to ask yourself again: 'What will the moderator give me marks for?'
- You must remember that you are writing about one particular faith – Christianity.
- You need to show that you understand what is important to Christians. What do they believe? How do their beliefs affect what they do?
- In some parts of the assignment you will be asked what you think. Make sure you show that you understand both sides of the argument – you will get more marks for this than for just giving your own point of view. Even then your own opinion is important.

Writing your assignment

- It is a good idea to begin each part of your assignment on a separate piece of paper. If you do, you can work on the different sections in any order you like. If you make any mistakes you may not have to rewrite quite as much.
- Marks are given for spelling, punctuation and grammar. Be careful to avoid mistakes.
- You must use your own words. Do not copy long passages straight from a book. A good idea is to read the passage, close the book, then write out what you want in your own words. Open the book again and check that what you have written is accurate.
- Use the correct religious terms. For example, Baptists use a baptistry, not a water tank.

Using illustrations

It is usually a good idea to use illustrations, as long as they are relevant to the assignment and you are able to explain how they are relevant.

When you have finished

- Your teacher will give you a coursework cover sheet. Fill it in carefully. You may want to practise with a photocopy.
- At the end of the assignment you should make a list of the books you have used. If you have had any help from someone other than your teacher, say so.
- Read the assignment again carefully. Check that you have answered all parts of the question.

Abba Aramaic word children used when speaking to their fathers. It means, literally, 'Dad' or 'Daddy'

Absolves pronounces forgiveness in God's Name

Adoration loving and worshipping God

Advent the period from the fourth Sunday before Christmas until Christmas Eve – a time of spiritual preparation for Christmas

Angel a spiritual being, believed to act as a messenger of God

Annunciation the angel Gabriel's announcement to the Virgin Mary that she was to give birth to Jesus

Apostles people sent out to spread the gospel, particularly the disciples of Jesus

Apostles' Creed a statement of belief based on the teaching of the Apostles and containing the basic principles of the Christian faith

Apostolic Succession the belief among the Episcopal churches that the authority of the holy orders of bishops, priests and deacons has been passed down from the time of the apostles

Ascension the Christian festival that takes place 40 days after Easter. It celebrates Jesus' return to the Father in heaven

Baptism to dip in water or pour water over someone as a sign of admission into the Christian community

Baptistry a sunken pool where believers' baptism takes place. In some churches, the area round the font

Believers' baptism the baptism of those who are old enough to make their own decision

Bible the holy book of Christians

Bishop the highest of the orders within the Apostolic Succession, with authority to ordain others to the ministry

Body of Christ the Christian Church is often known as this

Breaking of Bread the name given to the service of Communion by some Free Church Christians

Cardinal a high ranking bishop in the Roman Catholic Church appointed by the Pope and second in rank to him

Chalice the cup used for wine during services of Holy Communion

Charismatic worship worship that is free, lively and spontaneous, where the worshippers believe they are inspired by the Holy Spirit

Chrism a sweet-smelling oil used in baptism

Chrismation a ceremony of anointing with oil (chrism) immediately following baptism in the Orthodox Church

Christmas the time of celebration of the birth of Jesus Christ, God the Son

Church when written with a small letter c, it refers to a place where Christians worship; when written with a capital letter C, it refers to Christian people; it may mean a particular group of Christians or all Christians

Communion of saints the fellowship of Christians both on earth and in heaven

Confession an admission of having done something of which one is ashamed, accompanied by a wish to be forgiven

Confirmation a ceremony at which Christians who have been baptized make publicly their own promises of faithfulness to God; if they were baptized as infants they accept the promises made at their baptism by their parents and godparents; they receive the gift of the Holy Spirit

Congregation people who belong to a particular place of worship; people gathered for worship

Conservatives people who believe the Bible was inspired by God but is not a scientific text

Consubstantiation the belief that at the Eucharist the bread and wine become the body and blood of Christ while in no way ceasing to be bread and wine

Covenant an oath, a binding agreement and promise

Creed a statement of beliefs

Cremation the burning of a body to reduce it to ashes

Crematorium a place where cremations take place

Crucifixion death caused by being fixed to a cross; Christians think above all of the crucifixion of Jesus

Day of Atonement the most solemn day of the Jewish year; a day to ask forgiveness of God for sins committed

Deacon in some Free Churches, someone who assists in church worship and in administration. In Episcopal Churches, the lowest of the orders within the Apostolic Succession

Dedication a service in which a child is brought to the Church and the parents commit themselves to bringing up the child as a Christian

Divine Liturgy the Orthodox name for the Eucharist

Dogma a certain teaching of the church recognized by a formal pronouncement by the Pope

Easter the celebration of the resurrection of Jesus

Ecumenical universal, relating to things Christians of many tradtions do together and the beliefs they share

Electoral College cardinals of the Roman Catholic Church who elect the Pope

Encyclical a letter from the Pope to all Roman Catholic people, stating his opinion or rule on a specific subject

Epiphany the festival when Christians think of Jesus, God the Son, being made known to the world

Episcopal a system of Church leadership that is made up of bishops, priests and deacons

Eucharist the name given to a service of Communion; it means 'thanksgiving'

Ex cathedra means 'from the chair'. It is used especially of statements from the Pope in his position as head of the Roman Catholic Church, regarding faith and morals

Extempore prayer a prayer that is spontaneous, coming from the thoughts and feelings of the worshipper

Fellowship meal a meal shared by Christians as a sign of their shared faith in Jesus

Fundamentalists people who believe that the Bible was completely inspired by God and cannot contain errors

Funeral a service, held shortly after a person has died, to mark the end of that person's life

Gentile someone who is not a Jew

Good Friday the day when Christians remember the crucifixion of Jesus

Holy Communion the taking of bread and wine in Christian fellowship

Holy Spirit the third person of the Trinity; Christians believe the Holy Spirit is always with them, giving them strength and support

Holy Week the week before Easter during which Christians remember the events leading up to and including the crucifixion and burial of Jesus

Hymns songs of worship

Icon a religious image of Jesus, Mary or one of the saints

Iconostasis a screen in an Orthodox church separating the congregation from the altar and decorated with icons of Jesus, Mary and the saints

Incarnation God becoming fully human in Jesus Christ

Infallible/infallibility incapable of error

Infant baptism baptism of children who are too young to understand the commitment involved in baptism

Instituted began a custom

Intercession to ask something, usually in prayer, for someone else

Jesus Prayer a prayer that concentrates on the name of Jesus

Kingdom of God where God's greatness and authority are accepted; Jesus taught that it exists not only in heaven but also in the hearts of his followers

Last Supper the meal that Jesus shared with his disciples on the night before he was crucified

Lay people Christians who are not ordained ministers

Lent the time of preparation for Easter

Liberals people who believe that, most importantly, the Bible contains spiritual truth

Light of the World Jesus called himself the Light of the World in John 8: 12; Christians see him both as the one who shows them the Father and as the judge who can see the secrets of their hearts

Literalists fundamentalists who believe in the exact literal interpretation of the scripture

Liturgical worship worship that follows a widely accepted set order of words and actions

Liturgy a regular form of service, especially the Eucharist

Liturgy of the Word the part in a church service when passages are read from the Bible

Lord's Prayer the prayer Jesus taught his followers to say

Lord's Supper the name given to the taking of bread and wine in some Free Churches, such as the Baptist Church

Magi the Wise Men who visited Jesus

Magisterium the teaching authority of the Roman Catholic Church

Marriage a lifelong union between a man and a woman, which forms the basis of family life

Mass the name given to the Eucharist by Roman Catholics and some Anglicans

Means of salvation that through which Christians can be saved from their sins; in other words, the death and resurrection of Jesus

Mediatrix a person who mediates, pleads to God for other people

Meditation to think deeply, to reflect

Messiah the Hebrew name for the promised leader sent by God ('Christ' is the same word in Greek)

Ministry spiritual leadership

Non-liturgical worship worship that does not follow a widely accepted set order of words and actions

Ordained authority for a particular role within the Church through the laying on of hands by a bishop or other senior minister

Ordination a ceremony in which a person is given authority for a particular role within the Church through laying on of hands

Original sin the idea that all people are born with a weakness in their human nature, which makes them likely to sin

Parousia the second coming of Jesus

Paschal candle a large candle that burns at all services between Easter and Ascension; the five wounds of the crucified Christ are marked on the candle and at a baptism, a candle is lit from the Paschal candle as a symbol of the light of Christ

Passover Jewish festival celebrating the Exodus, the escape from Egypt

Penance a short prayer or other task undertaken to show sorrow and repentance for sins committed

Pentecost the Christian festival that takes place seven weeks after Easter; it celebrates the coming of the Holy Spirit to the disciples of Jesus

Petition to ask something, usually in prayer, for oneself

Pilgrim one who makes a journey to a holy place

Pilgrimage a journey to a holy place

Prayer talking to God; conversation with God; a form of words used when people speak to God

Preaching proclaiming and teaching the Christian faith; giving a sermon

Priest a person who is given authority through ordination to bless, absolve and celebrate the Eucharist

Prophet someone who speaks the will of God, a messenger

Psalm a sacred song or hymn

Pulpit the area in a church where preaching takes place

Rosary a set of prayer beads used mainly by Roman Catholics; a prayer is said as each bead is held in turn

Repentance to be sorry for your actions or sins; to turn away from sin and make a fresh start

Resurrection a restoring of life after death; the word refers to Jesus' returning to life after his crucifixion. It also describes Christians coming to life in heaven after they have died

Rite words and actions of an act of worship

Sacrament a rite or ritual (e.g. baptism) through which the worshipper receives a special gift of grace, a spiritual gift from God

Sacrifices offerings to God

Sermon a speech in which someone explains some aspect of the Christian faith

Service an act of public worship

Sins thoughts or actions that go against the will of God

Stations of the Cross a series of fourteen pictures that can be found on the walls of Roman Catholic and many Anglican churches, each station representing an event in Jesus' final journey to the cross

Testament one of the two parts into which the Bible is divided. The Old Testament was written before the time of Jesus and the New Testament was written by followers of Jesus. The basic meaning is 'a binding agreement'

Testimony a brief account given by a candidate for believers' baptism, outlining the experiences that have led them to request baptism

Transubstantiation the belief that at the Eucharist, when bread and wine become the body and blood of Christ, there is a change in the nature of the bread and wine

Trinity God the Father, God the Son, and God the Holy Spirit – three persons but one God

Vatican II a General Council of the Church (1962–5), which made pronouncements on many matters of Roman Catholic faith and practice

Vocation a feeling of being called to perform a task for God

Votive candles in Roman Catholic and some Anglican churches, Christians place a lighted candle near a statue of Jesus, Mary or one of the saints; the candles symbolize the prayers worshippers are offering to God for themselves or other people

Vows solemn promises that should never be broken

Worship praising and praying to God

Index